A PORTRAIT OF
JULIUS EVOLA

An Introduction to the Spiritual Traditionalism
and Modernist Critique of Julius Evola

LENNART SVENSSON

978-1-7638613-1-2

*A Portrait of Julius Evola: An Introduction to the
Spiritual Traditionalism and Modernist Critique of
Julius Evola*

Lennart Svensson

Thema Classification: QRYC (Esoteric Traditions),
VX (Mind, Body, Spirit).

MANTICORE PRESS
WWW.MANTICORE.PRESS

CONTENTS

Introduction..5

1. Evola and Italy.. 11
2. Biography.. 17
3. A General Outlook on Evola's Thought 33
4. Evola as an Artist and Poet............................ 43
5. Absolute Man 53
6. Pagan Imperialism.. 65
7. Revolt Against the Modern World 85
8. The Mystery of the Grail................................ 93
9. The Doctrine of Awakening 99
10. Men Among the Ruins................................... 105
11. Ride the Tiger... 139
12. Meditations on the Peaks............................... 149
13. Metaphysics of War 159
14. The Mindful Evola 169
15. *Gravitas, Dignitas, Contemptus* 177
16. Parallel Lives: Evola and Jünger 183
17. Coda: Tradition...191

18. Marginalia...195

Sources.. *199*

Literature... *201*

Appendix One... *203*

Appendix Two... *205*

Index of Persons.. *207*

About the Author.. *209*

INTRODUCTION

Julius Evola (1898 – 1974) was an Italian writer and thinker whose contributions have left an indelible mark on intellectual history.

His three most significant achievements can be summarized as follows: Firstly, he transformed Nietzsche's concept of the superman into a more spiritual and mindful archetype, known as the Absolute Man (*L'Individuo Assoluto*). Secondly, he offered a rigorous interpretation of Hindu philosophy, one that diverged from the more lenient approaches typical of the 20th century. Lastly, he provided radical conservatism with a doctrinal foundation rooted in ancient history, connecting our heritage to the polar and northern regions rather than the conventional Levantine and Middle Eastern origins. These elements encapsulate the essence of his doctrine.

Characterizing Julius Evola is no simple task. Perhaps he could be seen as a latter-day d'Annunzio, a readable right-wing Italian, or as Italy's Ernst Jünger, the archetypal radical conservative of their respective nations. However, Evola was both more and less than these figures: he did not write novels, and thus, one never encountered him through charming narratives about life, love, history, and myth, as seen in works like *The Flame of Life* or *Heliopolis*. Where d'Annunzio and Jünger were surpassed by Evola was in his stylish interpretation of myth and early history through the lens of Hyperborea and the polar-northern tradition. He enveloped us in the captivating winds from Agartha and Śambhala, from Prester John and Melchizedek, elements largely unknown to the mainstream of Western thought.

Julius Evola never achieved mainstream recognition, yet his influence has persisted discreetly even after his death. Since the 1990s, there has been a resurgence of interest in his work, with reprints of both his major and minor works becoming readily available through online bookstores. While he may never attain bestseller status in the conventional sense, his intellectual impact continues to be felt today.

This book aims to portray Julius Evola in a comprehensive manner. Like other contemporary authors on Evola, I delve into his ideas, but I also strive to present a readable narrative. While I do not offer new insights into the 'biographical Evola,' I have taken the time to explore his various facets, including his visual art and poetry. My ambition extends beyond the typical focus on 'Fascism and modernism' to highlight the ancient Evola—the polar, northern, Hyperborean aspect of Primordial Tradition that underpins his doctrine. This dimension is often overlooked in contemporary presentations of Evola, where the controversial aspects of the 20th century dominate, leaving little room for the truly captivating elements of his work.

This book, in its entirety, aims to present a comprehensive view of Julius Evola's intellectual legacy. While his political views are acknowledged, the focus extends beyond to encompass the broader worldview he espoused. This includes the concepts of Tradition, the Grail saga, polar symbolism, and a revolt against modernity. It delves into the notions of dharmarāja, chakravartin, and pontifex maximus. All these elements, along with references to cultural figures like Sergio Leone, are explored within these pages.

Therefore, I assert that this book is neither a piece of propaganda nor a sermon advocating any particular political ideology. While it is true that Evola championed 'Tradition' as a counter to 'modern thought,' which may render him controversial in certain political circles, I must clarify that I, as the author, have no interest in partisan politics. I am a free individual in a modern democracy, exploring subjects with an open mind and occasionally writing books about them, a practice I have engaged in for over a decade. The impetus for this book was simply my desire to write it. In other words, this is not an 'official Evolian statement,' if such a thing could even exist. This work is a sincere effort to portray a man who offered a thoughtful alternative to modernity, and who did so in a largely accessible manner.

Even when limiting my scope to the traditional and spiritual aspects of Julius Evola, I do not merely replicate his views and opinions. Instead, I offer my own interpretation of his standpoints and occasionally venture into spiritual realms that Evola, despite his proximity to Buddhism, never explored.

Moreover, Evola's own autobiography, *Path of Cinnabar*, primarily focuses on his official achievements and publications, offering little insight into his personal life. Consequently, portraying his life in detail is challenging. Nevertheless, I have compiled the available information and endeavored to present it in a coherent and engaging narrative.

To add a personal dimension to my work, I studied Indology at the University of Uppsala in the 1990s. Immersing myself in the traditional culture of India, learning Sanskrit, and decoding the Bhagavad-Gītā and other primordial texts provided me with greater wisdom than merely studying history, philosophy, and the history of 'Western thought,' the commonly lauded curriculum of the Humanities. *Hindutvā* and *Sanātana dharma* were far more captivating. However, contemporary academic Indology often focuses on extracting 'objective lexical meanings' from these texts, adhering to the ideals of 19th-century philology. Thus, Indology itself did not guide my quest for wisdom. Neither did new age interpretations or 'Hindu renaissance' presentations of the *Hindutvā* tradition. It was only in the 2010s, upon discovering 'the Traditional School' with figures like Guénon, Schuon, and Evola, that I began to view my Indology studies in a new light. This perspective allowed me to construct a credible alternative to modern thought, free from both supernatural sensationalism and academic narrowness. It transcended theories and ideas, leading to primordial forces and states, all illuminated by the eternal light, *Lux Aeterna*.

The Evolian perspective revealed to me a deeper path of wisdom, transcending the intellectual confines of 18th and 19th-century thought. It affirmed my inclination towards Eastern wisdom, for which I remain profoundly grateful. This personal journey and appreciation for Evola's guidance form the foundation of my motivation for writing this book.

Härnösand 26 September 2024

LENNART SVENSSON

CHAPTER ONE

One of my favorite anecdotes from ancient Roman wars involves the general Marius, who was besieging a castle. He challenged the enemy commander inside the castle, saying,

> 'If you're such a great general, come out and fight me.'
> To which the besieged commander replied,
> 'If you're such a great general, make me.'

This anecdote, sourced from Plutarch's *The Life of Marius*, illustrates tactical wisdom rather than providing specific insights into Marius himself. The broader context was Marius's effort to quell a significant insurrection across Italy, known as the Social War around 90 BCE. The entire Italian peninsula rebelled against Roman rule, not to establish an Italian kingdom or republic, but to gain equality with Roman citizens. By the end of the Social War, Italians had achieved the privileges of Roman citizenship.

This period marked the nascent stages of Italian nationalism and the concept of a unified Italian state encompassing the entire peninsula, often referred to as the 'Italian boot.' The human symbol of Italy, the mythical *Miss Italia*, depicted as a young woman with a mural crown (*Italia turrita*), was already present in antiquity, as seen on Italian stamps. During the Republican and Imperial eras, Rome incorporated Italy as its imperial heartland, not as a separate administrative unit. Despite this, the idea of Italy persisted as a vague concept. The personification of Italia, the striking woman with a spear and crown, continued to exist in a shadowy form. It was not until the medieval period, in the twilight of the empire, that Italy began to emerge as a distinct entity.

Italian nationalism began to take shape with figures like Dante, a classically trained scholar who chose to write in the vernacular Italian language rather than Latin. His *Divina Commedia*, a monumental journey through Hell, Purgatory, and Heaven, remains a symbol of his achievement and is still widely read today. The idea of unifying the Italian peninsula gained momentum with scholars like Machiavelli in the 1500s, who urged his patron to lead the movement for a united Italy. This sentiment is reflected in the dedication of his treatise on realpolitik, *The Prince*, where he implores the Prince of Medici to be the leader of the unification movement, rallying under the cry, *"insieme – unite, unite, Italy!"* While Machiavelli did not state this explicitly, it encapsulates the essence of his thought.

However, liberation was still a distant dream. For many centuries, Italy remained under the yoke of foreign rulers, including the Austrians, Spanish, and Papal authorities. The late 1700s brought the French Revolution, a triumph of secret societies plotting to overthrow the old regime, which also had an impact on Italy. Italy had its own secret societies, such as the Carbonari. Initially, under Napoleon, Italy endured foreign occupation and serfdom, with France looting many of its artistic treasures accumulated since antiquity. However, following the peace of 1815, France was compelled to return the stolen artifacts. With the assistance of these rebellious societies, Italy eventually emerged as a united land, forming a unified kingdom.

This period was known as the *Risorgimento* – the resurgence. It marked an essential transition. The time of distinct duchies, provinces, and dominions that constituted Italy until then had to come to an end.

Although the chapter might be titled 'Evola and Italy,' his ideas were not significantly influenced by concepts such as 'Italy,' 'Renaissance,' and 'Risorgimento.' While Evola was Italian by birth and lived most of his life in Italy, his spiritual foundation did not primarily stem from Italian history. Instead, he drew inspiration from the Roman Empire and its founder, Julius Caesar, which is why he chose to spell his first name as "Julius" in the Latin form, rather than the Italian "Guilio."

Evola represented values such as *Romanità, gravitas, dignitas,* and *contemptus* – gravity, dignity, and contempt – specifically in terms of disdain for the masses, as well as conventional Italian conservatism and nationalism.

His inspiration was Julius Caesar. The Shakespearean portrayal of Caesar aligns closely with Evolian ideals. The protagonist's declarations, such as "I am constant as the northern star" and "I am not afraid to tell grey-beards the truth," epitomized the grandeur of Italy's and Rome's past, which greatly influenced Evola. In contrast, figures like Machiavelli, Garibaldi, Mazzini, and Cavour, notable Italian heroes from more recent history, did not resonate with him. Nevertheless, he held a certain regard for the House of Savoy, the royal family that governed unified Italy from 1861 to 1946. To Evola, a crowned monarch symbolized a connection to Tradition.

Evola was a Mediterranean male deeply influenced by ancient traditions, including those of the Northern-Āryan variety. He displayed indifference, and perhaps even hostility, towards certain spiritual authorities in Italy, specifically the Papacy and Christianity in general. Evola referred to Christianity as "the religion that came to prevail in the West," which was a factual and diplomatically phrased description, without any spiritual endorsement implied.

Evola exhibits a distinct stance among Italians. While many Italians identify as atheists or have secular beliefs, Evola's opposition to Catholicism is notably more pronounced. He championed the Hyperborean tradition, which is not a widely recognized belief system. However, this tradition could gain recognition due to his influence, as well as that of René Guénon, who significantly impacted his views.

Evola supported a tradition associated with the Grail sagas, Āryan Hinduism, and Greco-Roman, Celtic, and Nordic mythologies. He promoted a patriarchal, northern, solar belief system in contrast to a southern, lunar, gynocratic one. He advocated for sun worship in mountain temples over moon worship, silvicultural rites, and orgies. Evola emphasized Āryan northernness and order during times of disorder. He provided a foundation for radical conservatism that extends beyond historical figures such as Spengler and Nietzsche, rooting his beliefs deeply in history and mythology.

The Hyperborean myth is suggested to be significant for our time. According to the succession of Yugas, we are currently in the ascending Dvāpara Yuga, also known as the mindful bronze age, which aligns closely with Evola's teachings. Although he did not recognize that the Kali Yuga had ended, his final recommendation, *Ride the Tiger*, corresponds well with the transition from a materialist era to a more esoteric period.

For these reasons, Evola's perspectives warrant consideration. His teachings offer relevant insights for contemporary times.

CHAPTER TWO

Mindful Beginnings

G*uilio Cesare Andrea Evola* (1898-1974) was an Italian philosopher, artist, and occultist. Born in Rome to Sicilian parents (Vincenzo Evola, 1854-1944; Concetta Mangiapane, 1865-1956), Evola distanced himself from his Christian upbringing and adopted a freethinking approach. Early influences on Evola included Otto Weininger (1880-1903) and Friedrich Nietzsche (1844-1900). He described his routine as spending days in the library, adhering to a structured yet self-determined reading schedule [Evola 2009, p. 8].

Evola developed an interest in Futurism and subsequently met the movement's founder, Marinetti. However, their relationship deteriorated due to differing viewpoints. Specifically, Marinetti was an Italian patriot, whereas Evola envisioned Italy's future in alignment with Germany.

Evola served as an artillery officer during World War I, although he experienced limited combat. Nevertheless, his service in the Italian Alps sparked a lasting interest in mountain climbing, which became a lifelong passion.

After the war, Evola faced significant challenges. His pre-war perspective and lifestyle lost their relevance. This is discussed in *Path of Cinnabar*. He used drugs and experienced mental distress. He even contemplated suicide. However, his robust health and some inspiration from Buddha helped him recover. In the words of Evola:

> I reached such a low point that I had planned to bring my very life to an end – I was about twenty-three at the time. I only avoided such an outcome – the very outcome which, in different ways, both Weininger and Michelstaedter had ruinously embraced – thanks to something that I might almost describe as an enlightenment: my discovery of an early Buddhist text (*Majjhimanikāyo* I.1). [Evola 2009, p. 15]

In this original, hard-core Pāli Buddhist text, the Buddha speaks about reaching transcendence by avoiding attachment to the world, and all bonds – both spiritual and material. This includes thoughts of "extinction." As the Buddha says: "He who takes extinction to be extinction and, having taken extinction to be extinction, thinks of extinction, thinks of extinction, thinks of extinction, thinks

'Mine is extinction', and rejoices in extinction, such a person, I say, does not know extinction." Evola was inspired after reading these words, and wrote that,

> These words struck me as a sudden ray of light. I then felt that my urge to leave and to dissolve myself was merely a bond, a form of 'ignorance' contrary to true freedom. At that moment, I believe, a change took place within me, and I acquired steadfastness capable of overcoming all crises. [ibid p. 16]

Subsequently, Evola ceased using drugs, having recognized that their primary function is to activate latent aspects within oneself.

Interwar Years

In the post-war period, Evola dedicated himself to painting and poetry. He was closely associated with the Futurist and Dadaist movements, although he was not as prominent as key figures like Marinetti and Tristan Tzara, whom he met. However, he eventually abandoned painting and poetry to focus on his career as a philosopher and writer.

During the 1920s and 1930s, he dedicated himself to writing articles, pamphlets, and books. He resided in Rome, often with his mother, at Corso Vittorio Emanuele No. 197. This apartment was located in an upscale building, exhibiting a palatial façade. Positioned east of the Tiber River in central Rome, this residence was within a one-kilometer radius of notable historical landmarks such as the Pantheon, Trevi Fountain, Castel Sant'Angelo, Roman Forum, Quirinal Palace, Palatine Hill, and Janiculum Hill. These surroundings epitomize the History and Tradition that Evola came to represent.

During the interwar years, Evola was part of the sophisticated social circles in Rome. He had a relationship with the writer Sibilla Aleramo (1876-1960) and also associated with the Russian occultist Maria de Naglowska (1883-1936). This suggests that he appreciated the company of women, indicating that Evola had a heterosexual orientation.

In *Meditations on the Peaks*, Evola discusses traveling to the Alps for various holiday trips. During the 1920s and 1930s, such activities were typically associated with the affluent lifestyle of the elite and upper middle classes. Evola himself was an aristocrat with a noble background. He was known for wearing a monocle and was likely financially independent due to inheritance.

Fascist Challenge

The main event shaping Italy in the 1920s was Fascism. Evola was not involved in the Fascist movement as a party member, nor did he hold any official position during the Fascist regime. As an intellectual, he criticized some aspects of its doctrine.

However, he expressed a preference for Fascism over Socialism and Conservative Catholicism.

In the early 1920s, Italy was experiencing significant turmoil. Prior to Mussolini's rise to power in 1922, the nation faced immediate chaos and long-term stagnation. The chaos was primarily attributed to socialist and communist activities allegedly influenced by foreign elite groups. Long-term stagnation was rooted in historical issues such as corrupt politicians, a weak parliamentary right (influenced by the Pope discouraging the Christian phalanx from political engagement), the unresolved tensions between the papacy and the Italian state, an ineffective military, economic stagnation in southern Italy, local patriotism known as 'Campanilism' (where the area within the sound of the church bell, *la campanile*, constituted one's whole world), and inadequate representatives of the royal court.

According to Swedish writer Göran Hägg (2012), the Fascist movement ascended to power with the assistance of a political establishment that had reached an impasse. For some, the Fascists seemed to be a more manageable and less threatening option compared to the Communists. In 1922, Fascism emerged as a uniquely Italian response to Italy's specific issues at that time.

Despite nuances, Fascism experienced a period of acceptance among European political elites. For example, in the 1920s, Churchill remarked that if he were Italian, he would have supported Mussolini—a revealing statement indicative of that era before alliances crystallized in the late 1930s. One of Fascism's fundamental aspects was militarism, emphasizing military conquest, an area in which Fascism ultimately failed. It was overshadowed by Nazi Germany, its ally from 1939, within this realm. Furthermore, as previously noted, Evola, while not a member of the Fascist movement, recognized some of its promising elements, such as the admiration for ancient Rome. Nevertheless, he also critiqued Fascism for its empty modernism and lack of spiritual grounding.

Legionary Spirit

In March 1938, Evola visited Romania. During his time in the capital city of Bucharest, he met both Mircea Eliade and Corneliu Codreanu on the same day. Eliade was recognized as a distinguished scholar of religion with profound spiritual insight, while Codreanu was known as a right-wing radical with strong Christian beliefs.

Evola appears to have been significantly influenced by Codreanu. In the preface to Evola's *Men Among the Ruins*, H. T. Hansen writes: "Codreanu ... was definitely one of the very few indisputable 'heroes' and models for Evola. Everything he wrote about him amounted to a panegyric." [Hansen 2002, p. 80]

Codreanu served as an ideal for Evola. Hansen, for example, recounts the situation in 1943 when Mussolini had just been rescued and reinstated by German forces. Supporting Mussolini was not Evola's primary concern; however, he was inspired by the "legionary spirit" he encountered in Romania, which emphasized loyalty above all else.

World War Two

As we revisit the period during which Evola experienced World War II, it is necessary to go back briefly to recount an event from 1939.

Based on research by Dana Lloyd Thomas, Hansen [ibid] states that in 1939, Evola attempted to join the Italian Fascist Party by submitting an application. It is suggested that Evola did this with the intention of serving as a volunteer in the anticipated war.

"Evola wanted to serve as an officer, as he had in World War I, and this was possible only if he became a party member." [p. xiii] They declined his request because, in various writings, Evola had criticized Fascism, and he had been demoted in 1934. The context was that Evola had refused to duel with a reporter he had criticized in La Torre; both Evola and the reporter had backgrounds as officers, and the authorities believed military rules of honor should apply, which traditionally involved dueling. But Evola, traditionalist as he may have been, "was against the duel because he did not want to place himself at the same level with this man whom he later described, along with other journalists, as an 'authentic gangster'. The proceedings over this were finally brought before a military court, which ruled against Evola and demoted him." [ibid]

1943 Crisis

In the summer of 1943, the Allies were advancing towards Italy. Having expelled Axis forces from North Africa and Sicily, their next objective was the Italian peninsula. From the Italian perspective, the situation was marked by uncertainty and a lack of clear direction: Would Italy remain an ally of the Axis powers, declare neutrality, or join the Allied forces? The Italian population was notably war-weary; however, severing ties with Nazi Germany posed significant risks and challenges.

The situation peaked in July 1943.

Rome was bombed by the Allies for the first time on 19 July 1943. This event turned Italian public opinion against Mussolini. Several members of the government also opposed him, leading to the summoning of the Fascist Grand Council for the first time since the war began. In the council meeting held on 24-25 July, top Fascists united against Mussolini, resulting in his removal and detention. King Victor Emmanuel appointed Marshal Badoglio as the new head of the government.

On 3 September, the Allies initiated an invasion of the Italian mainland in the south. Subsequently, later in September, German forces occupied northern Italy and established the Fascist Salò Republic. Finally, on 13 October, the principal Italian government in Rome, under the Badoglio regime, aligned itself with the Allies.

Evola Goes to Germany

Evola documented his observations from the summer of 1943 until the American entry into Rome on 5 June 1944 in a diary. To summarize, we can describe Evola's situation in the late summer of 1943 as follows.

Following Mussolini's fall, Evola was approached by members of the German Embassy, with whom he had a long-standing collaboration, to consider relocating to Germany. Although Evola had previously visited Germany numerous times and was regarded as a notable guest in the Third Reich, he declined the invitation. He perceived himself as a neutral observer and had not held any official positions within Fascism nor joined the Party. As an independent observer and writer, his aim was to advocate for what he believed was in Italy's best interest. Evola's rapport with certain radical-conservative factions in Germany afforded him a precarious form of protection, at least temporarily.

He decided to stay in Italy, specifically in Rome, to observe the events of the coming days. However, the situation remained precarious. The Badoglio government officially maintained its alliance with Germany while simultaneously attempting to negotiate an exit from the war through secret discussions with the Allies. Evola anticipated this development in his diary, noting the improbability of an anti-Fascist Italy, having ousted the Duce and repudiated his ideology, continuing to combat the global anti-Fascist coalition in such an ideologically driven conflict.

Evola had contact with the German diplomatic community in Rome. After the fall of Mussolini, there was an assumption that the Badoglio government could be trusted as an ally. However, the SS sent Otto Skorzeny to Rome with his commando unit, dressed in Luftwaffe uniforms to avoid suspicion. There were rumors about a coup to remove Badoglio and establish a regime more aligned with Nazi interests. Such a coup required Italian cooperation and a figurehead who might compete with German interests. As a result, it was decided to free Mussolini and install him as the head of state in the north. These considerations led to Mussolini's liberation from Gran Sasso d'Italia in mid-September 1943, which was executed by Otto Skorzeny's raid.

In late August, Evola received an invitation to travel discreetly to Berlin to discuss Italy's situation.

On this occasion, Evola concurred and proceeded northward. Accompanying him were an officer, a journalist, and a squadrist who remained loyal to Mussolini. According to Evola's own account, the journey unfolded as follows [for the online source, see Sources]:

> Our journey was not devoid of colourful incidents. We went separately to Bolzano, to a given inn, to the concierge of which we gave an agreed password. On the strength of this we were put in contact with local elements of the SD, who were waiting for the arrival of a military bus which was to cross the border. We got onto it, putting on military coats and German caps, and passed rapidly through the Brenner border post, whose guards did not venture to stop German military cars, especially if they were 'Waffen-SS'. We reached Innsbruck, and from there we continued to Berlin by train. On the way, we just escaped an air raid. We had to remain for a long time in front of the bombarded city. Once we had entered it, we found a degree of chaos among the people who had been waiting for us, since a bomb had hit a part of the building where the offices of the SD dealing with the Italian sector were located. – To avoid attention (I, in particular, had many acquaintances in Berlin), we were accommodated in the main Potsdam inn. Days of meetings and contacts followed, during which an attempt was made to examine, from the point of view of the

Axis, the most urgent problems posed by the Italian situation. Once again, the divergences between the circles of the SS and those of the career diplomats, prone to optimism or, at least, to the wait-and-see policy, appeared. However, I did not want to over-extend my absence from Italy, for various reasons, mainly because of the need to assess any possible developments in the situation and to find out whether new forces were gathering. My friends and those who accompanied me had already gone back, and I was ready to leave, when the Auswärtiges Amt, that is, the Foreign Office, which had finally heard of our mission, informed me that the Minister Giovanni Preziosi wished to see me. Because he was particularly exposed, owing to his various campaigns inspired by Fascist intransigence and his absolute faith in the Axis, Preziosi, with the help of the German Embassy in Rome, had left Italy, and was at this time living incognito, together with his wife and son, in Bad Reichenhall, near Munich. I readily agreed to meet him before going back to Italy. This was the occasion which was to lead me to visit Hitler's General Headquarters, and to see Mussolini again just after his liberation.

In early September 1943, Evola departed from Italy and traveled north to Nazi Germany to discuss the new political landscape. Accompanying him were several Fascists, including Vittorio, the son of Mussolini. Their objective was to develop a conceptual framework for a new Italian state that would continue to fight alongside the Allies.

For instance, the group was escorted to East Prussia and Hitler's headquarters. On 14 September, Mussolini himself arrived, having just been liberated from his Gran Sasso prison by Otto Skorzeny.

The plans devised by these Italians, under German supervision, effectively laid the groundwork for what would become the Salò Republic, the Fascist regime established in northern Italy. It appears that Evola did not play a significant role in these discussions, nor did he meet the Führer.

Subsequently, Evola returned to Rome. He was able to do so relatively safely as the city had been occupied by German forces since 8 September 1943. To protect the historic city, its inhabitants, and its buildings from the ravages of war, the Pope declared Rome an *open city* in accordance with the Geneva Convention of 1864. The atmosphere of this period is vividly depicted in the film *Rome – Open City* (1945), which tells a grim story of military rule.

Evola remained in Rome until the end of German rule. He might have believed he could live undisturbed under an Allied occupation government. However, he had to leave the city and move to Germany again.

Fall of Rome

Rome was captured by Mark Clark's Army on 5 June 1944. Evola was present in the city on that day, and subsequently, the situation became critical as Allied Intelligence began searching for him. They arrived at his residence where he lived with his mother; she detained the agents at the entrance, allowing the philosopher to exit discreetly through the back door.

In his suitcase he primarily had this: the manuscript that would eventually become the three-volume Introduction to Magic (*Introduzione alla magia*).

Evola departed the city on foot and soon encountered retreating German troops, ensuring his safety. With connections in Austria, Evola decided to proceed to Vienna, where he subsequently engaged in research on Freemasonry for the Sicherheitsdienst (SD), the Nazi intelligence agency.

Fateful Day

On 21 January 1945, Evola experienced a significant incident. During an air-raid by American bombers in Vienna (not Russian, as his memoir holds), he chose not to seek shelter and instead was walking outside, engaging in his usual practice of testing his stoic endurance during such raids. Near Schwarzenbergplatz, a bomb detonated, and the resulting shock wave caused him to be thrown against scaffolding. Upon awakening in a military hospital, he was informed that he had sustained a spinal cord injury, which resulted in partial paralysis from the waist down. Despite extensive stays in various hospitals and clinics, this condition persisted. Nevertheless, he was able to return to Rome and live on a disability pension.

In 1952, Evola was visited by associates, including anthroposophists Massimo Scaligero and Giovanni Colazza. During this meeting, they observed Evola moving his legs slightly, which surprised them. This was not unusual as he was only partially paralyzed.

The End

Evola lived with his mother until her death in 1956, after which he lived alone, likely in the same apartment on Corso Vittorio Emanuele.

On June 11, 1974, Julius Evola passed away while seated at his desk, gazing out of the window towards Janiculum. In accordance with his last will, he declined a Christian burial. His ashes were instead placed in a glacier crevice on Monte Rosa, part of the Pennine Alps mountain range.

CHAPTER THREE

An overview of the key concepts and attitudes of Evola is essential. Hence, we present this chapter. The primary source will be H. T. Hansen's foreword to *Men Among the Ruins*, an analysis of Evola's thought. While Hansen does not extensively discuss Evola's traditional inclinations, this summary will address that aspect as well. Thus, this chapter provides a comprehensive understanding of Evola's perspectives on political doctrine, philosophy, and Tradition.

It is widely acknowledged that Evola held right-wing and radical conservative views. However, it is important to examine the specific nature of his right-wing ideology and the form of radical conservatism he supported.

One might start by noting that Evola was described as "antidemocratic (though not at all anti-liberty)" [Hansen p. 99]. This distinction is one of many important nuances in understanding Evola's philosophy.

Further, when defining the nature of Evola's general political stance, Hansen says this: "[Evola] is not really fighting against Bolshevism, Americanism, and consumer culture, but rather against contemporary man." [p. 102]. The essence of Evola's philosophy focuses on the individual, or rather the "person," not any silent majority, metaphysical people, or collective entity like the Russian "mir." In the Western tradition, it is the solitary individual who must contemplate the world and take a conceptual stand after thorough analysis. While this may lead to over-intellectualizing and sterile thought exercises, it is also an honest and analytical approach. As an individual within this framework, challenges are seen as opportunities to overcome. The modern world presents obstacles, which are then addressed and managed by strategically utilizing its own dynamics, akin to *riding a tiger* until it becomes manageable and control can be assumed.

This demonstrates the intellectual valor of Evola, which will be further discussed in Chapter Four under his concept of *superomismo*.

Germanophile Predilection

A significant aspect of Evola's thought is his attitude towards Germany, which may be even more relevant than his views on Italian Fascism and Italy.

Early on, Evola was pro-German, advocating for Italy to fight on Germany's side in 1914 according to the then Triple Alliance of Germany, Italy, and Austria. According to Hansen: "Evola had developed a sympathy for Germany during World War I that set him at odds with his Futurist friends. Later he developed the idea of the unification of the 'two eagles' – the German and the Italian – based on the Ghibelline notion of Empire during the Hohenstaufen period." [ibid p. 58] His interest in Germany was intellectual and somewhat detached. As a person deeply connected to Mediterranean culture, he did not resonate with the *völkish* movement, Nibelungen-romanticism, or Wagner.

During World War II, Evola aligned with the Axis powers of Germany and Italy. He frequently traveled to Germany for lectures and had support in German radical conservative circles.

Evola's interest in German culture led to interactions with Heinrich Himmler's organization, the SS. Evola was invited to deliver lectures to SS leaders in 1938. However, Himmler was cautious of Evola and his intentions. A staff report from Himmler's office described Evola as a "reactionary Roman" who longed for the feudal aristocracy of old and opposed modernity. The report recommended that Evola should not receive support and be prevented from further speaking engagements in Germany. Himmler agreed with these conclusions in August 1938. This information is based on Hansen's foreword to *Revolt Against the Modern World*, 1995, p. xviii.

Evola, who had a strong affinity for German culture, found himself in a precarious situation. It was uncommon for an Italian to express admiration for Germany; even Mussolini, despite his significant dependence on Germany, privately harbored critical views towards Germanic matters. Furthermore, official representatives of Germany, including Himmler, did not want Evola operating in their country, as his teachings were incompatible – and even hostile to – the Third Reich.

Evola's German friends continued to support him, and his books, such as *Rivolta* and *Pagan Imperialism*, were translated and praised by some critics.

Tradition

It is possible to regard Evola as an *intellectual figure.* He resided in a city, engaged in writing and reviewing books, and critically analyzed various doctrines and cultural elements. In fact, he was highly critical, expressing disdain for modernity and non-traditional aspects. Furthermore, he opposed much of mainstream conservatism and new age attitudes.

Primarily, he expressed a significant disapproval of the modern world. He harbored certain grievances, akin to those of contemporary writers. Nonetheless, he never identified himself as an "intellectual." He aspired to transcend that designation, seeking to be more than merely a journalist influenced by newspapers and conventional education. Therefore, he should perhaps be regarded as a magician or what he termed a "magical idealist," a concept he adopted from Novalis' *magical idealism.*

His engagement with Tradition, Tantra, and other Eastern doctrines, as well as the polar concepts of Paradesha and Thule, the Grail sagas, and the Eddas, along with his emphasis on "the purity of heroic action," suggests that he should be regarded as more than just a 20th-century intellectual. He may be considered a magician, prophet, or shaman of visual and poetic art. He represents an archetype of the Absolute Man, Total Man, or Magician Man.

Evola had a powerful charisma, somewhat like a sorcerer. Mussolini viewed him as a shaman or evil magician, reportedly making the "gesture of the Evil Eye whenever he [Evola] was mentioned." [Hansen p. 49]

German Gestalts

Everyone on the right knows about Nietzsche and Spengler. So now we ask ourselves: how was Evola influenced by these two?

This is what Evola got from Nietzsche [ibid p. 12]: the strain of being *anti-Christian, anti-bourgeois, anti-contemporary prejudices.*

The same source [p. 15-17] indicates that Spengler influenced Evola to adopt a critical perspective on modern civilization. Spengler emphasized the importance of a more dynamic culture, beyond just "mere work, mere necessity" – advocating for a culture focused on heroes rather than submissive individuals. Hansen also notes that Evola translated and wrote an introduction to Spengler's *Decline of the West,* and contributed to the Italian edition of *Jahre der Entscheidung.*

Despite their differences, Evola found Nietzsche's essentially anti-spiritual nature to be a significant point of contention. Nietzsche represented a persistent challenge to Evola, compelling him to continually define his own position in opposition. This indicates the considerable impact Nietzsche had on Evola. Regarding Spengler, however, Evola stated in his autobiography that "Spengler's writing influenced me in no way" (Evola 2009, p. 206).

Guénon

René Guénon, the French mystic and scholar, was the primary influence on Evola's intellectual development.

As a young man in post-World War I Italy, Evola already had an inclination towards esotericism. In *Arte Astratta*, he advocated for an art that originated from within the artist. Additionally, he found in

Buddhism a doctrine that emphasized the mindful individual. Evola was also interested in "magical idealism" and had speculated on the concept of the "Absolute Individual."

Therefore, the traditional, religious, and spiritual atmosphere of Guénon's work resonated with him. Despite not adhering to Guénon's theistic beliefs, Evola readily embraced the mystical perspective presented by Guénon. This perspective placed man's origins not in the Middle East, as perennial thought had traditionally done, nor in ancient India, as some believed, but rather in Hyperborea, a region in the polar area during the last interglacial period.

Guénon did not specify any particular time period for the foundation of his "Hyperborean tradition." However, he described a human past situated in the polar region, referred to as *Midgard, Paradesha, Thule,* Śveta-Dvīpa, *Ariyanem Vaejah,* which suggests a northern origin for humanity's spiritual history. This concept forms part of Guénon's ideas, which influenced Evola's thought. This provides a reference point for these ideas that is difficult to challenge.

The Hyperborean strain is often regarded as a traditionalist myth or a conceptual utopia of antiquity. It can be likened to science fiction in its use of abstract concepts to create a narrative of remarkable beauty and scope. However, it is not merely an exercise in rhetoric. Evidence from ancient Chinese, Hindu, Persian, Middle Eastern,

Greco-Roman, Celtic, Nordic, and Amerindian sources suggest a belief in human origins in polar, northern regions, envisaging an entire polar continent. This culture is depicted as one of light, golden splendor, and divine influence, providing a counter-image to a chthonic, southern, lunar, and female-oriented religiosity.

When Evola first encountered Guénon's writings, he disagreed with him, particularly on the true meaning of Vedānta (see Chapter Fourteen). However, they eventually found common ground in their belief that human origins lie in traditions much older than commonly thought. This is Evola's portrayal of Guénon's ideas as described in *Path of Cinnabar:*

> First and foremost, Guénon was engaged in a serious and detailed analysis of what he termed 'traditional science,' as well as in an exposition of myth and symbolism that took account of supra-rational and 'intellectual' elements – in such a way as to distinguish itself from both the so-called comparative study of religion, and from the kind of study once pursued by Romantics and pursued today by psychoanalysts and irrationalists. Guénon was always keen to emphasize the 'non-human' character of such wisdom: this is what helped me to distance myself from profane culture once and for all, and to recognize the futility of any attempt to establish some sort of foundation and point of reference for 'modern thought'. [Evola 2009, p. 97]

Evola, in his books, refers to "the world of Tradition" as a standard for evaluating everything. This concept is derived from Guénon, who used Tradition as a positive counterpoint in his critique of modernity. In *Cinnabar*, Evola mentions that Guénon pointed to a "Hyperborean" origin as the source of this Tradition, describing it as inspired by a "non-human" element. The term "non-human" may seem unusual to Western readers, who are accustomed to human-centric expressions like "man is the measure of all things." However, "non-human" in this context means "above human, suprahuman," implying something "divine or godly."

The Sanskrit term that Guénon references for a "non-human" perspective is *apauruṣeya*. According to Evolian terms, a world based on Tradition represents "the fundamental structure behind all organic, differentiated, and hierarchical civilizations – civilizations in which all spheres of influence and human activities are ordained from above and directed towards it." [ibid] This form of Tradition suggests a structured system with enduring values, as opposed to the modern world, which is characterized by its mechanical and urban nature.

Evola embraced the concept of Tradition with remarkable enthusiasm, integrating it seamlessly into his previous theories and perspectives as detailed in *Cinnabar*. His notion of the Absolute Man could initially appear as a lawless rebel. However, when this superman descends from the realm of ideals and abstractions to engage with concrete historical realities, the concept gains tangible vitality. The Absolute Man can then exercise *power*, manifesting in the form of priest-kings, solar warriors, and authoritative figures of traditional civilizations, such as the *dharmarāja, the chakravartin, the pontifex maximus,* and legislators akin to Manu.

In conclusion, it can be stated that the Nietzschean concept of the "aristocrat of the soul" assumes a more enduring, historical (or "meta-historical") significance when reflected upon within the framework of Tradition.

This chapter's discussion will be revisited later in this study, with particular emphasis on the Hyperborean element. This serves as an introduction to Evolian thought.

CHAPTER FOUR

Evola started painting in 1915, initially influenced by Futurism and later by Dadaism. However, it is challenging to categorize his paintings as strictly "Futurist" or "Dadaist." To better understand his overall artistic style, it can be noted that he was predominantly *an abstract painter.* "*Arte astratta*" was a recurring theme in his work.

In the early 1920s, Evola was involved in painting, writing essays on art, and participating in exhibitions. In 1923, he gradually became more interested in philosophy and mysticism, leading him to stop painting. He later resumed painting, though it was of less significance. During his youth, abstract painting was a significant focus for him for a few years.

Evola is regarded as a significant abstract artist with spiritual inclinations, drawing parallels to contemporaries such as Wassily Kandinsky and Johannes Itten, both of whom were associated with the German Bauhaus school. This spiritual element is evident in Evola's work *Arte Astratta*, written in

1920, likely his first publication. In this essay, Evola proposed that "art is selfishness and freedom," suggesting that it serves as a spiritual means of self-expression, enabling the artist to enter a trance-like state and transcend individual limitations. According to Evola, the artist must delve into his inner psyche to create "interior landscapes" and should eschew realist approaches like "research" and "observing the outer landscape." Simply painting scenes relatable on a human level is deemed superfluous.

Moreover, Evola wrote that: "Modern art will fall soon, and this will be the sign of its purity. It will fall, moreover, because it has been created with a method from the *outside* / because of a gradual elevation of sickness over partly passionate reasons / rather than *from the inside* / mystically."

In conclusion, visual art should emphasise interiority. Evola regarded the artist's work as a guiding light in a world overshadowed by darkness.

> Abstract art may never be historically eternal and universal: this, *a priori* – PLOTINUS, ECKHART, MAETERLINK, NOVALIS, RUYSBROEK, SVEDEMBORG [sic], TZARA, RIMBALD [sic] … all of this is but a brief, rare and insecure lightning through the great death, the great nocturn reality of corruption and disease. In a similar way, it is the rarity of unspeakable gems among the enormous muddy Ganges. [quoted after the ebook-version, see Sources for details]

In *Abstract Art*, Evola challenges traditional art and the notion of the artist as an inspired genius. This perspective presents some issues, as it suggests that the divine influx guiding artists may have become outdated in the post-WWI context. While traditional art, encompassing figures such as Dante, Wagner, Beethoven, and various realist and romantic painters, had grown comfortable with its established methods and Renaissance-Baroque-Classicist orientation, it failed to critically examine the essence of art itself. There was an assumption that masterpieces could be created merely by adhering to established conventions. Consequently, a renewed sense of introspection was necessary.

Art was becoming standardized and predictable. According to the pamphlet: "the principles of practice, nature, and feeling represent the result of spiritual inertia. Every truth ... is comfort." Evola suggested that contemporary thinking often lacks depth; we must explore beyond traditional boundaries into multidimensional space, surpassing identity and causality, to discover new possibilities.

Necessity does not govern all aspects. Artists should move beyond psychology and rationalism to understand themselves. Philosophy alone cannot achieve this; it requires "intimacy and solitude, duty and power." A broader understanding than a mechanistic explanation of the world is necessary.

Modern metaphysics, as interpreted by Kant and Hegel, often overlooks the unique existence of the individual self. It is suggested that a different approach to knowledge is needed. Modern science has not significantly contributed to the understanding of the concept of the ego, and its technological advancements are deemed irrelevant.

Contemporary and historical art are perceived as lacking spirituality. Therefore, it is proposed that art needs to be rethought with an abstract method that emphasizes purity and freedom. This approach contrasts with scientific methods, emphasizing that true creativity comes from illumination and grace. Art is seen as embodying selfishness and freedom, and extensive research is viewed as detrimental to the essence of art.

While Evola might critique the concept of creativity itself, he also opposes the notion of an artist being merely a glorified scientist. This perspective aligns with creators like American performer Laurie Anderson, who avoids research in her artistic process, exemplified by her statement, "I never do research. I'm an artist," and her song "Oh Superman," which can be related to Evola's views.

In discussing his artistic philosophy, Evola references Schönberg and Tzara as true geniuses, rather than Wagner and Dante. Instead of genuine perception, an anti-method is proposed: "to place oneself in nothingness, coldly, under a very lucid and surgical will." This represents true creativity characterized by selfishness and freedom. Evola's associate, Marinetti, also understands this concept. Rhetoric and sentimentality, along with sincerity, good faith, and inspiration, must be abandoned. Instead, self-denial is advocated, described as the "drowning of the personality to infinity." Abstract art serves as the medium for this process. It is through a cold, steely will that immortal art is created, surpassing the doctrine of "naturalness, sentiment, and humanity."

Romantic expression, represented by figures such as Goethe, Hugo, Beethoven, Wagner, and Keats, is often characterized by sentimentality that must be controlled. The new spiritual art should employ *Verfremdung*, which involves distancing oneself from the motif to better understand its essence; this is a concept familiar to true artists. J. G. Ballard referred to it as the "death of affect as an approach to character." Artworks should be created with a Stoic *apatheia*, leading to disinterested art that is "devoid of any usual content": pure expression and form, where form and content coincide, similar to music.

This is the Evolian proclamation of abstract art. In this initial public presentation of his ideas, the elements of his later advocacy are already evident: no reference to God and the soul, yet with an emphasis on interiority, individuality, spirituality, and infinity. A consistent theme is his critical stance towards the Renaissance and subsequent movements such as Romanticism. He would never rely on them as foundations for his worldview. For better or worse, this represents "the eternal Evola," the established and steadfast Evolian creed. Although his creed was not fully developed in 1920, he had laid its foundations – a non-Christian, non-academic, and non-romantic, yet esoteric Weltanschauung.

The "Interior landscape"... is a recurring title for some of Evola's artworks, and it gives us the essence of abstract art. It is not about painting everyday landscapes (Constable, Corot, Dahl), not even about deforming the motif (impressionism, Gaugin, Picasso, Matisse); instead, it is about painting what you see with your inner eye (François Nomé, C. D. Friedrich, Moreau, Böcklin). It is Goethean: "alles vergängliche is nur ein gleichnis" – *all that we see in the everyday world are just similes.*

Therefore, focus inward and seek to connect with eternal images, with *eidoi*. Reflect on your inner landscape, and depict what you observe. This approach aligns with the Evolian philosophy of abstract art.

Evola's abstract artworks intentionally exhibit a certain roughness and ungainly feeling. The aim was not to evoke sweet emotions or charm; beauty was not the objective. Instead, the intention was to create an edgy, disconcerting atmosphere that aligns with reality. This approach, known as *Verfremdung* and alienation, aims to bring viewers closer to the message of the work by providing a more sober perspective.

The same can be said about Evola's poems.

During his years as an abstract painter, Evola also wrote poetry. His poems are known for being enigmatic and challenging. They can be described as abstract art in literary form.

Evola's poems do not gently lead the reader to the conveyed vision. They do not offer a pleasant experience as traditional poems generally do. Unlike Eliot and Pound, who referenced traditional elements to provide relatability in modern, form-free poetry, Evola's work aims to evoke an alienating feeling of perplexity, or *Verfremdung*. When reading Evola's poems, one frequently asks, "what does this mean...?" Any meaning may be present but is obscured by dense layers of meticulously crafted lines, such as this:

> In harbours the dressed galleys and the splendours will sink in the outer darkness – the door shuts behind us ... Life is algebra and the plants absorb the metal with their sap ... its veins are thin threads of crystal ... in the city the lights are shut ... automatons in trucks carry away the dismal corpses ... life is algebra and pumica and the plants absorb a lot of metal with their sap ... my friend you will dream when it snows ... 999 cubic root Shanghai.

This information can be found in "The Obscure Dialogue of the Inner Landscape," which was published in 1920 as part of a Dada anthology printed in 99 copies. For the online source, please refer to the section titled "Sources."

Here is another example of Evola's poetry. This excerpt, from a poem in *Arte Astratta* titled "opus 32 – theme and variations," has been translated into English by Olivia Sears (details provided below in Sources):

a gallop of low clouds pregnant with terror // makes your head spin // gallop gallop // silent sobs of distant blue-green soft rosy-pink lightning in the distance // a slow parade of black beasts crosses my diaphanous heart // an immense shadow should hang over everything // over everything // ghostly windmills are turning // and the sky is dead // and this atmosphere charged with apocalypse above all the little pink things, delicate, unconscious // such silence

Another poetical excerpt from *Arte Astratta* is this one, "dreams":

> some are laden with velvet and venom
> immense immobile desolate lunar dreams
> on the nostalgic prairies that nurture them
> and lithe lilac dreams that cling to ecstasies
> the tepid virgins move to the terraces
> and the people of the great high spheres move
> toward golden domes

Evola subsequently abandoned both painting and poetry. Nevertheless, the stylistic skills he developed as a poet proved beneficial in his career as an author, albeit implicitly. His writings exhibit a distinct style, which is more pronounced than that of René Guénon, who otherwise had a significant influence on Evola's ideas.

His painter's eye also served him well in painting landscapes in literary form. This can for instance be seen in his essays about mountain climbing, which we will discuss later.

CHAPTER FIVE

In the introduction, it was stated that one of Evola's significant achievements was enhancing Nietzsche's concept of the superman with greater mindfulness. *L'individuo assoluto* is the term Evola uses to refer to this being.

What, then, can be said about this mindful superman?

This concept is challenging to explain in a straightforward and transparent manner, as Evola does in works such as *Path of Cinnabar*, due to the inherently complex nature of the subject. It is better understood intuitively; Nietzsche himself recognized this by presenting his concept of the superman through a novel form, as seen in *Thus Spoke Zarathustra*. Additionally, Nietzsche often conveyed his thoughts through aphorisms in his essays. Following this approach, we will provide a textual collage that aims to present the idea of the Evolian Absolute Man. We hope that the combined elements will create a comprehensive understanding that exceeds the sum of its parts.

Absolute Individual

The idea of the *L'individuo assoluto...* refers to the concept of action as being, according to Evolian philosophy: "Every externalization of the interior awakens a deeper interiority."
(*Fenomenologia dell'individuo Assoluto*)

In *Dark Star Rising: Magick and Power in the Age of Trump*, Gary Lachman describes the concept of the "absolute individual" as possessing "the ability to be unconditionally whatever he wants." Lachman elaborates further: "For Evola, the 'absolute individual' is a condition of self-awareness that perceives the identity of itself and ... Will. For him, 'I' *am* the will become conscious." This idea can also be related to Max Stirner's work, *The Ego and its Own*, which is said to have influenced Rudolf Steiner's writing of *The Philosophy of Freedom.* These works explore themes of individuality, freedom, and the perception of reality, emphasizing the potential to create the world anew.

Evola was influenced by German idealist philosophy. However, this philosophical tradition often overlooks the role of the individual and his will. Evola therefore redirected his focus to the individual, emphasizing his connection to "the divine" or the

Absolute. This led to the concept of the Absolute Man, Total Man, or Magician Man. "Absolute Man" is a self-reliant superman, embodying Total Man and Magician Man, destined for the glory of a *Sonnenmensch divya.*

Nietzsche inspired this perspective. Evola adapted Nietzsche's superman concept, elevating it beyond mere vitalism to connect with higher realities. He argued that merely worshiping life isn't enough; something more transcendent is needed. This was discussed in *Borderline.*

Aristocratic Radicalism

Nietzsche profoundly influenced Evola to aspire beyond his existing self, to become a transcendent *superuomo.* The grandiose ambition of transcending the ordinary, coupled with a transcendent attitude, resonated deeply with Evola. It was characterized by "the pitilessness, without caring about himself" (Hansen), complemented by a caustic linguistic style. The objective was to become an elitist aristocrat of the soul.

Evola already possessed an aristocratic demeanor, identifying himself as a baron with noble ancestry, often donning a suit and monocle. He sought to elevate this aristocracy to a philosophical and existential dimension. Therefore, Absolute Man's actions take on a mythical quality, a concept

Evola inherently understood. Like Nietzsche, he recognized the necessity of stylizing oneself both in words and actions. "Hierarchy, spirituality, and order" – this encapsulates Evola's philosophy of mindful supermanism.

Aham Brahmāsmi

Evola wrote an autobiography titled *The Path of Cinnabar*. In the chapter "The Speculative Period of Magical Individualism," he discusses his concept of the Absolute Individual.

This approach seeks to render Nietzsche's concept of the superman, and indeed all of existentialist philosophy (including thinkers like Sartre and potentially Heidegger), with greater mindfulness. The quintessential existentialist appears disoriented in this world; whereas the Absolute Man, conversely, is guided by his own will. He exhibits an exceptionally strong will, surpassing any other force in the universe. Through willpower and vision, he recognises his own spiritual strength.

Heidegger discussed the concept of individuals being "thrown" ("Geworfen") into the world. In contrast, Evola disputed this viewpoint, suggesting that people are exactly where they are supposed to be, as determined by their karma.

This represents the concept of the Absolute Individual, an enlightened version of Nietzsche's superman. Nietzsche's superman is given a spiritual dimension, connected to inner and hidden realities, similar to the "aham brahmāsmi" in Hindu philosophy, which translates to "I am God". The mindful superman can assert this "devoid of any sinister or titanic overtones" [Evola 2009, p. 71]

Evola's concept of the Absolute Man combines the serene Hindu ātman with the introspective European self, creating a new spiritual *superomismo*. By using terms such as the Absolute Man, Total Man, or Magician Man, Evola asserts dominion over each moment, claiming it for his transcendent self. The Absolute Man recognises the divine light within himself, elevating his state through *influxus* to achieve a higher existence.

Superomismo

Absolute Man avoids both the fervent Nietzschean philosophy and the pessimism of 20th-century existentialism. Nonetheless, the existentialist perspective that one must actively live one's life rather than construct an ideal morality theoretically is adequately reflected in Evolian thought. Evola criticizes the "academic" idealism of philosophers such as Descartes, Hegel, and Kant, often referring to it as "professor philosophy for philosophy professors" [Evola, 2009, p. 34].

Despite acknowledging its limitations, Evolian superomismo represents a significant doctrine within European thought concerning a conscious form of supermanism. No other philosopher has succeeded in extricating Nietzsche's ideas from the pitfalls of materialism, emotionalism, and nihilism as effectively as Evola.

For an Evolian critique of Nietzsche, refer to *Borderline.* To examine an Evolian appreciation of Nietzsche, consider his remarks in *Pagan Imperialism:*

> Freeing the doctrine of Nietzsche from its naturalistic part, we see that the "overman" and the "will-to-power" are not true except as supra-biological qualities and, we should say, supernatural qualities, then this doctrine, for many, can be a path by which the great ocean can be reached – the world of the solar universality of great Nordic-Āryan traditions, from whose summit the sense of all the misery, of all the irrelevance, and of all the insignificance of this world of the shackled and maniacs imposes itself. [Evola 2017, p. 86]

Evola grants the individual absolute authority by recognising an Absolute Self. He revitalised esoteric thought following the decline it faced after Nietzsche's proclamation of "God is dead," as well as the rise of utilitarianism, logical positivism, and Darwinism. Evola's approach involves avoiding mere vitalism and instead seeking that which transcends life. This requires the individual to discover hidden, inner spiritual forces within his own being.

Evola instructs that an individual is essentially a "god in being," perceived as an absolute entity – an Absolute Man. The phrase "aham brahmāsmi" or "I am" invokes this dimension within the individual.

Absolute Man liberates the individual from relying solely on discursive thought for solving problems, instead guiding them to an understanding where reality is conveyed through symbols and myths. Rationality and analysis are not sufficient on their own; intuition and emotion are also essential for navigating the complexities of modern life. This perspective was advocated by Evola from the 1920s onwards.

In other words, intuition takes precedence over discursive rationalism. Evola's thought aligns with the supra-rational perspectives of Plato, Plotinus, Schelling, Schopenhauer, Heidegger, and Jünger. Hansen describes Evola's ideology as "a supra-normal self-realization centered on transcendence" [Hansen, p. 7].

Overcoming the Human Condition

Evola presents a perspective that transcends the limitations of human existence. The adage "man is the measure of all things," attributed to an ancient

Greek philosopher, represents a reductionist view lacking spiritual depth. Conversely, Evola advocates for the transcendence of the human condition. He emphasizes the importance of seeking the divine within oneself and upholding "supra-personal and supra-temporal values."

Once again, the term *apauruṣeya* comes to mind. The doctrine that guides and elevates humanity is beyond human origin; it is divine.

Evola viewed Tradition as encompassing more than human aspects; it represented a means to achieve "immanent transcendence" through a non-human, or divine, force embodied in leaders, such as in the concept of divine kingship. Tradition manifested itself in objective and supra-personal legislation.

Our considered commentary is that few, if any, Western thinkers of the 20th century have had the boldness to deny the sanctity of the individual, or "the ordinary person." Evola's approach advocates for individuals to exceed their current state and strive to realize their fullest potential—transcending the mundane, everyday *alltäglich*, "human condition." Evola asserts that there is more to humanity than mere "humanism." By stating, "we have to overcome the human condition," Evola provides guidance on how to move beyond an emotionalist, reductionist, and myopic perspective.

"I have said, Ye are gods"...

Absolute Man is *sovereign*. Evola himself employed this term. As an interpretation, one could observe this sovereign status of the individual exemplified in Evola's own experiences during World War II.

While acknowledging some exaggeration, it can be said that Evola, despite his Italian heritage, emerged as a figure of sovereign authority, embodying a unique force. This was accomplished through his self-assurance and understanding of *"aham brahmāsmi,"* recognizing himself as the Absolute Man – the Complete Man – the Magician Man.

The mindful superman embodies everything.

He transcends conventional morality but is not devoid of ethical consideration. Possessing an inherent sense of discernment and guided by his "daimonion" (inner voice), he can differentiate between right and wrong. However, he does not require moral precepts to inform his actions, nor does he adhere to established pathways such as the noble eightfold path or the Ten Commandments. This pragmatic approach to morality is demonstrated by Evola in *Ride the Tiger*.

Similarly, supermanism is intuitive; however, it is neither anti-rational nor irrational. Rather, it is *supra-rational*.

The superman operates with mindfulness, driven by willpower rather than desire. This does not imply an absence of preferences; in specific situations, he is aware of his objectives. He performs necessary actions with pragmatism, capable of analyzing operational contexts rationally and acting accordingly.

This concept, which aligns with the idea of "having god within" (also known as *aham brahmāsmi*), serves as the fundamental principle of *Ride the Tiger*. Interestingly, it also coincides with the ancient Germanic Asatru creed.

Evola had some knowledge of the Eddas and Germanic wisdom, but he was not considered an authority on these subjects. His perspective was more aligned with Roman traditions. However, as demonstrated in his work *Ride the Tiger*, he successfully captured the essence of what scholars such as von List, Gorsleben, and Serrano have articulated about the ethics of the Germanic people. This wisdom is formally unstructured (lacking ten commandments or a specific noble path), yet it is neither random nor arbitrary. It embodies an intuitive and pragmatic approach, suggesting that any individual who possesses the ability to think, to strive, and recognizes his inner divine potential, can aspire to be a superman.

As previously mentioned, Evola presents a concept of mindful supermanism characterized by fierce determination. This superman lacks pity and is unconcerned with self-interest in the conventional sense. He is an ascetic who has renounced worldly attachments, severing all ties in pursuit of inner perfection. He is described as "advancing with a devouring fire that leaves nothing behind itself" [Evola 2003, p. 51].

CHAPTER SIX

PAGAN IMPERIALISM

One of Evola's pivotal works is *Imperialismo Pagano.* The German translation from 1933 was titled *Heidnischer Imperialismus,* and the English version, published in 2017, was named *Pagan Imperialism.* Notably, this English translation was based on the German edition.

Pagan Imperialism was first published in 1928, during a period when Fascist Italy was on the verge of signing the Lateran Treaty with the Vatican. Evola criticized what he perceived as the "maternal and lunar" nature of Christianity and advocated for a more "masculine and solar" belief system for Italy. Additionally, he expressed dissatisfaction with Fascism, regarding it as overly bourgeois. Furthermore, he opposed the entire complex of Communism, Liberalism, and democracy.

Pagan Imperialism is an essay by a traditionalist author. It has a more assertive tone compared to *Revolt Against the Modern World,* which is often considered his major work.

Rivolta is presented as a detailed lecture about esoteric subjects. *Pagan Imperialism* conveys similar ideas as *Rivolta*, but with more emphasis and style. This aspect is significant in terms of readability and stylistic appeal, which are not always prominent in Evola's books. Raymond Chandler's advice to the author was "the word is *gusto*," and *Pagan Imperialism* aligns with this approach to writing.

We will examine *Rivolta* too, but first, we will focus on this somewhat neglected Evolian work, *Pagan Imperialism*.

Almost all of the themes that Evola later explored in his works are present in his book, *Pagan Imperialism*. These themes include the importance of hierarchy, the advocacy for a "polar, northern, solar" tradition in contrast to the "southern, lunar, female" tradition associated with Abrahamic religions, and the call for a more thoughtful interpretation of Nietzschean philosophy. Additionally, Evola emphasizes the grandeur of Imperial Rome and the Holy Roman Empire, the necessity of a philosophy that transcends mere vitalism, and the pursuit of essential truths – encapsulated by the phrase "life, and more than life."

In *Pagan Imperialism*, the Roman idea and the ancient Roman example are highlighted instead of the concept of "Tradition" found in Evola's later works. He discusses notions such as "a revived Dorian simplicity". [Evola 2017, p. 82] To Evola, Rome in this essay represents the organism (as opposed to the simple aggregate); the spiritual (rather than the materialist); everything accomplished by rite and symbol; and truth (instead of empty rhetoric).

Pagan Imperialism speaks about a "will to order and to hierarchy, to virility, and to authority". [p. 96] This is Evola's ideal.

Additionally, Evola discusses the necessity for a new group of leaders in his book. These leaders should be responsible individuals capable of making significant sacrifices. They should possess inherent leadership qualities, demonstrate a willingness to risk their lives in fulfilling their roles, and not merely engage in empty rhetoric.

He discusses the importance of shifting from a materialistic approach to science to one that explores spiritual and internal aspects, aiming to understand and manage the deeper forces that influence our existence.

He talks about replacing dependence and lack of will with sufficiency; equality ideals with *difference, distance, hierarchy, aristocracy.* Pure will and absolute action are prioritized over "love" and happiness.

Evola suggests that the new rigorism will envision a life where every moment is an act of heroism. The ideal individual in this new era is referred to as Absolute Man, Total Man, and Magician Man.

A Rebel Fighting for Tradition

Pagan Imperialism lends itself to extensive quoting. We can, for instance, look at the beginning [p. 6]. This is a call to arms for any radical traditionalist. These are words by "a rebel, fighting for tradition":

> The current 'civilisation' of the West is expecting a substantial upheaval, without which it is doomed to collapse sooner or later. – It has realised the most complete perversion of every rational order of things. – There is no longer breath, nor liberty, nor light in the realm of matter, of gold, of the machine, of number. – The West has lost the meaning of command and obedience. – It has lost the meaning of Action and of Contemplation. – It has lost the meaning of hierarchy, of spiritual power, of man-gods.

This is just the beginning, the rest is equally strong [ibid]:

> [The West] no longer knows nature. This is no longer, for Western man, a living body made up of symbols, gods, and ritual acts – a splendid cosmos, in which man moves about freely, like 'a kingdom within a kingdom': he has instead deteriorated into an opaque and fatal exteriority, the mystery of which profane sciences try to ignore with petty laws and petty hypotheses. – The West no longer knows Wisdom: it no longer knows the majestic silence of those who have mastered

themselves, the bright calm of the Seers, the superb 'solar' reality of those in whom the idea has become blood, life, and power. Wisdom has been supplanted by the rhetoric of 'philosophy' and 'culture', the realm of professors, journalists, and sportsmen – the scheme, the program, the manifesto. It has been supplanted by sentimental, religious, humanitarian contamination and the race of windbags who flounder and madly rush while exalting 'becoming' and 'practice', because silence and contemplation frighten them.

Evola discusses aspects of modern life, such as sentimentalism, moralism, and simplistic humanism. He suggests that these should be addressed [p. 8]:

To all this, let it be said: 'Enough!', so that some men may return to long-lasting paths, long-lasting risks, long-lasting gazes, and long-lasting silence; so that the wind of the open sea may blow again – the wind of the nordic primordial tradition – and arouse the sleepers of the West. Anti-philosophy, anti-humanitarianism, antiliterature, anti-'religion', this is the premise. 'Enough!' must be said to aestheticisms and idealisms ...

Evola aspires to transcend simple discussion and casual conversation [p. 9]:

In silence, through hard discipline, self-mastery, and self-overcoming, with tenacious and brisk individual effort, we must create an elite in whom 'solar' Wisdom is revived: that *virtus* which cannot be spoken, which rises from the depths of feelings and the soul and is not proved with arguments and books but with creative acts. – We must reawaken to a renewed, spiritualised, and austere sense of the world, not as a philosophic concept, but as something which vibrates in our very blood: to the sensation of the world as power, to the sensation of the world as rhythm, to the sensation of the world as a sacrificial act. This sensation will create strong, hard, and energetic characters, beings made of strength and then only of strength, open to that sense of freedom and nobility, to that cosmic breath which the 'dead' in Europe have babbled a lot about, yet have not even felt its puff.

Modern man requires a revival of sacredness, myth, contemplation, and seriousness: *gravitas* and *dignitas* [ibid].

Against secular, democratic, and material science, always relative and conditioned, slave to phenomena and incomprehensible laws, deaf to the deepest reality of man, we must reawaken – in this elite – the sacred, inner, secret, and creative science, the science of self-realisation and 'self-dignification', the science which leads to the hidden forces which govern our organism and are united with the invisible roots of rate and things themselves, and which creates mastery over these forces; so that, not as a myth, but as the most positive of realities, some men are reborn as beings who no longer belong to "life", but to "more-than-life", and are capable of transcendent action.

To guide man into this Brave New World of willpower and vision, a new elite and breed of leaders are needed [ibid]: "There will be Leaders, a race of Leaders. Invisible Leaders who do not speak and do not show themselves, but whose action does not experience resistance and who can do everything."

Nordic Symbolism

To achieve this regeneration of the West, we must turn our attention to the North. Evola addresses this concept in *Rivolta*, but provides a more concise and elegant discussion in *Pagan Imperialism* [p. 10-11].

> We alluded to a primordial Nordic tradition. It is not a myth, it is our truth. Indeed, in the most remote prehistory where the positivist superstition postulated right up until recently cave-dwelling ape-men, there existed a primordial, unified, and powerful civilization, an echo of which still resounds in everything that the past has to offer us as an eternal symbol. – The Iranians speak of the *Airyanem Vaejah*, located in the farthest North, and see in it the first creation of 'god of light', the origin of their lineage and also the seat of 'glory' – *hvareno* – that mystical force characteristic of the Āryan race, and especially of their divine

kings; they see in it – symbolically – the 'place' where the warrior religion of Zarathustra would have been revealed for the first time. – Correspondingly, the tradition of the Indo-Āryans knows the *Śveta-dvīpa*, the 'Island of Glory', also located in the far North where Narayana, the one who 'is the light' and 'who stands above the waters', that is, above the causality of events, has his residence. It speaks also of the *Uttarakuru*, a Nordic primordial race; what is meant by Nordic is the solar path of the gods – *deva-yāna* – and the term uttara connotes the concept of all that is sublime, lofty, and superior – of what in the figurative sense can be called *arya*, Āryan – according to the concept of 'Nordic'. – Again, the Achaean-Dorian stocks are heirs of the legendary Nordic Hyperboreans: the most characteristic god and hero of this race – the solar Apollo, the annihilator of the serpent Python – came from there; Hercules – the ally of the Olympian god against the giants, the annihilator of the Amazons and of elemental beings, the 'fair conqueror', of whom many Greek and Roman kings later considered themselves so to speak, as his avatars – would have carried the olive tree from here with whose branches the victors were crowned (Pindar).

Nietzsche Lauded

It is well-documented that Nietzsche had a significant influence on Evola. For example, as mentioned in

LENNART SVENSSON

Chapter Four, during the 1920s, Evola discussed the concept of the "Absolute Man" (*l'individuo assoluto*), which can be viewed as an evolution of Nietzsche's superman into a more contemplative entity. While Evola's major works often exhibit a critical stance toward Nietzsche, including in *Pagan Imperialism*, there are instances where he openly commends Nietzsche. An illustrative passage capturing the spiritual essence of Nietzsche's work is presented below; we previously cited part of this in Chapter Four, and here we provide a more extended excerpt [p. 85-86]:

> [T]hose who are still not capable on their own can find a precursor even in these dark times, someone misunderstood, who waits in the shadows: Friedrich Nietzsche. The Nietzschean experience is still not exhausted, since it has not even started. What is exhausted is the aesthetic-literary caricature of Nietzsche, conditioned over time, and theological-naturalistic reduction of some parts of his theories. But the value carried heroically by Nietzsche after much nameless suffering, in spite of the fact that his whole being revolted and yielded, until, without any complaint, after having given everything, it collapsed – this value which is beyond his 'philosophy', beyond his humanity, beyond himself, identical to a cosmic meaning, reflection of an economic force – the *hvareno* and the terrible fire of solar initiations – this value is still waiting to be understood and assumed by contemporaries. There is already

in it the call for arms, the appeal for loathing, for awakening – and for the great struggle: the one in which – as we have said – the destiny of the West will be settled: either to fall into twilight or enter a new dawn. – Freeing the doctrine of Nietzsche from its naturalistic part, we see that the 'overman' and the 'will-to-power' are not true except as supra-biological qualities and, we should say, supernatural qualities, then this doctrine, for many, can be a path by which the great ocean can be reached – the world of the solar universality of great Nordic-Āryan traditions, from whose summit the sense of all the misery, of all the irrelevance, and of all the insignificance of this world of the shackled and maniacs imposes itself.

Āryans held the sun in high regard and incorporated it into their worship practices. Julius Evola recognised this belief system and viewed the Nordic civilisation as epitomised by its royal and triumphant qualities. According to Evola, this type of civilisation is characterised by a victory of form over chaos, a superhuman triumph over human and telluric concerns, and an ideal of transcendent virility represented by solarity. This concept relates to the roles of sovereigns, heroes, and rulers within spiritual and material realms.

In ancient Rome, which practiced paganism, Northern solar influences were evident in symbols such as the Wolf, the Eagle, and the Axe. These influences were also manifested in the worship of deities like Zeus, Apollo, and Mars, who were characterized by their brilliance, majesty, and sternness. Additionally, this strain was reflected in a desire for eternity, the interweaving of action and ritual, and "in the crystal-clear and yet potent experience of the supernatural, which was acknowledged in the Empire itself and culminated in the symbol of Caesar as numen." [p. 13]

This is the key point we wish to emphasize in *Pagan Imperialism*. This succinctly introduces the ideas that Evola will further develop in *Rivolta*.

The Sacred in the Roman Tradition

Evola demonstrated a profound interest in Roman spirituality, the Roman approach to religious thought, and the Roman concept of sacrality. His work *Pagan Imperialism* extensively explores these themes. Around the same period, in 1929, Evola reviewed Vittorio Macchioro's book *Roma Capta. Saggio intorno alla religione dei Romani* (1928) in the *Ur* periodical. Evola's review was titled "Sul 'sacro' nella tradizione romana," which translates to "The Sacred in the Roman Tradition."

This paper highlights a significant aspect of Evolian thought: the emphasis on rite and ritual. This focus is somewhat uncommon, even within traditionalist perspectives. Historically, in Indology, Vedic religion devolved into an obsession with the mechanics of sacrifice. The exact execution of sacrificial rituals became more important than the spiritual connection with deities. Consequently, the brahmin conducting the sacrifice assumed a position of authority over the gods, controlling them through ritual practices. Similarly, the religiosity of ancient Rome encompassed an extensive series of actions and ceremonies related to sacrifices made to various gods and numina. However, this has not frequently been cited as a model for a viable religious tradition.

Evola stands out as one of the few individuals who approaches this matter with a ritualistic perspective.

We must avoid engaging in dualist polemics by labeling the phenomenon as "ritualism" and assuming a position of superiority. Instead, it is essential to examine the fundamental aspects of the matter. Evola himself references the etymological origin of the term "ritual" in the Sanskrit word *ṛta*. In Vedic times, *ṛta* signified the divine world order, which later evolved into the concept of *dharma*. Within Indo-European analysis, *ṛta* shares its root with Latin terms such as *rite*, *ritualis*, and *ritualus*; English terms like *rite* and *right*; German *Recht*; and Swedish *rätt*. *Ṛta* represents the rightful order of things, while *anṛita* symbolizes chaos and disorder. Therefore, by performing *ṛta*, one aligns with the divine order.

One might assert: the rite is *ṛta*, and *ṛta* is the rite. The rite constitutes an integral part of the rightful order of the cosmos. It represents a formal action grounded in being. By performing the rite, we establish a connection to being, serving as a virtual link between humanity and divinity.

The various types of rites and their methods of performance constitute a broad topic that we need not explore in depth. Evola himself does not address this matter extensively. One might assert that the rites of the past belong to history, at least in a formal sense. There is no necessity to revive the Hindu Horse sacrifice or the Roman *Souvetaurilia.* These were rites appropriate for their respective eras, now supplanted by other forms of sacrifices. Nevertheless, certain rituals remain essential. Humans invariably engage in them, even within secular or nearly secular contexts. We observe rites of passage, such as student examinations, marriages, and funerals. While these rites can be modernized and streamlined, it is impossible to escape their fundamental significance entirely.

How much more effective it is, therefore, to conduct rituals with solemn meaning, deliberate intent, and in a respectful manner.

Connecting with the divine involves more than reading about deities. Engaging in rites can reinforce this connection in a comprehensive manner, involving both body and soul. This concept was understood by ancient civilizations, where rituals and sacrifices played an essential role. While it is not feasible to revive traditional Indo-European rites such as the Horse sacrifice or elaborate Roman ceremonies, incorporating some form of ritual into our lives remains important. As Jünger once noted, we constantly perform rites and make sacrifices, often without realizing it.

This is how we understand the role of ritual, rites, and ṛta.

Evola shares a similar perspective on this matter.

For example, in the discussed text, Evola commended the Roman approach to engaging with the divine through *action* rather than mere contemplation. The Romans perceived the divine as "numen," an imperceptible force. As Evola stated: "The numen is the divinity conceived of not so much as a 'person' than as a 'power', a principle of action".

During the Roman era, ritual held a paramount place in the worship of deities. This practice was reminiscent of the ritualism observed in pre-Upanishadic Brahmanism. Roman religion did not pursue the search for 'truth' but rather focused exclusively on mastering the correct performance of rites.

Furthermore, "The conception of god as numen corresponds, in ancient Rome, to the conception of the cult as pure rite." Certain names of invocation were "*nomina agentis*," indicating they had a practical rather than mythological origin. The focus was on rites rather than prayers or dogmas. The Romans' interactions with the sacred were centered in ritual practice. According to Macchioro, they

> never had a theoretical or ethical or metaphysical content, it never possessed, and never wanted to possess, a whole of doctrines, either on God, or on the world, or on man; it exhausted itself in the rite. There was no religion, either good or bad, either true or false, outside the rite. To accomplish exactly the rite means to be religious. The one who alters the rite comes out of the limits of religion, and however pure and sincere his intention, falls into superstition.

The Roman approach to religion did not involve theoretical, ethical, or metaphysical content and did not aim to develop doctrines about deity, the world, or humanity; it concentrated solely on ritual practices.

Evola discusses the power of the rite:

> In a laboratory, by clumsiness or by imprudence, an experience can be spoiled. Then, it needs to be redone, if one has not suffered the consequences of the mistake, which the slightest thing can have been enough to cause. The same thing can be thought of ritual action.

Furthermore,

> According to Livy (XVII, 9) (1), after the
> terrible battle of Trasimene, it is not a priest,
> but a general, Fabius, who said to the soldiers:
> 'Your mistake is more to have neglected
> sacrifice than to have lacked courage or skill.'

Concluding with this:

> The one who does not manage to see the virile,
> dry splendour of that spirituality because
> any 'religious intimacy', any sentimentalism
> and any theological speculation appears as
> almost non-existent in that world made of
> numina and of riti, can be inclined to define
> the Roman vision of sacred as a 'magical
> primitivism', almost of savage peoples.

Ritualism involves the use of rites as a method.
It is important not to engage in name-calling.
The rite serves as a significant means of engaging
with the divine realm. In "action as rite and rite as
action" [*Pagan Imperialism,* p. 13], we gain a deeper
understanding of essential reality. Rites are always
performed, and sacrifices are made on altars, often
without conscious awareness. In secular contexts,
concepts such as "democracy, economic growth,
and freedom" are venerated. By acknowledging gods
through rites, the spiritual dimension is recognized.

One might state: the ritual imbues the entire body of
the individual performing it with profound mystical

wisdom. "Every externalization of the interior awakens a deeper interiority," as Evola said in his Absolute Man essay.

In Evola's *Saggi sull'idealismo Magico* it is stated: "Philosophy is the train of thought that finally sees into its own inadequacy and realizes the need for an *absolute* action that originates from within." [Quoted after Hansen, p. 29]. Being wise involves more than just being intelligent and well-read; it requires absorbing knowledge fully. A disciple gains wisdom not only by receiving information but also through actions that involve their etheric body.

It is imperative that we *anchor remembrance in the etheric body*. Castaneda mentions this concept as "remembering with the body." Additionally, at the beginning of Norman Stevens' *The Rainbow Warrior*, there is a quote from page 337 of Alice Bailey's *The Rays and the Initiations* which echoes this sentiment:

> The Mysteries are revealed, not chiefly by receiving information concerning them, but by the execution of certain processes, effected in the etheric body of the disciple. These cause him to know what is hidden…

In the essay "The Sacred in the Roman Tradition," Evola discusses the concept of immanence. The Romans integrated spirituality into their daily lives, with gods participating in everyday experiences. Unlike Greek religion, where the divine was transcendent and abstract, Roman spirituality was immanent. Evola states:

> Let us now come to another characteristic of the Roman conception of the sacred. Its 'immanence'. In this respect, one should not think of the speculations of 'idealist' modern philosophy. To explain ourselves, let us compare the style of Roman spirituality with the Hellenic one. Whereas the latter is mainly under a – let us put this way – spatial sign, the former is under a temporal sign. For the latter, the gods, objects of pure contemplation, live as eternal essences in the absolute space of the 'supraworld'; for the Roman, instead, the gods, without losing anything of their metaphysical dignity, manifest essentially – as numina– in time, in history, in human vicissitudes, and the greatest concern of the Roman was that of coming to a balance, of favouring an encounter between divine forces and human ones, or to see to it that these prolonged or channelled those. The whole oracular Roman art meets a similar idea; and since, in its turn, the weaves [Sw. *väv, material*] of the oracular answers and of the oracles was inseparable from the whole deeds of Romanity, it can be said that the whole Roman history assumed, for our ancestors, the character of a true sacred history, of a story adumbrated constantly by divine meanings, revelations and symbols. The fact is that all this did not have as a counterpart an ecstatic and passive attitude, but rather an active, warlike attitude.

It can well be said that the Roman made his history sacred, feeding forces into it and acting united with them.

A particular aspect of 'immanence' concerns the human symbol. It is well-known that, at the origins of Rome, the pontifical dignity and the royal one were gathered in one single person; even subsequently, and before the Augustean restoration, in the figures of the consuls and in many other typical Roman figures, sacred functions were essentially the prerogative of political leaders. Even more typical examples could be found in the specifically sacred domain. One of them was brought to light by Kerényi. In Hellas, it was the statue which symbolised, in its perfection and achievement, the Olympian god. In Rome, the same god had instead consecrated a living symbol, the *flamen dialis;* this majestic and pure figure, closely connected with the idea of the state, appeared throughout his life as a living symbol of the divinity – so that it could be called precisely "a living statue of Jupiter". And, even though in already crepuscular reflections, similar meanings maintained in the Imperial epoch. The imperial cult is precisely a testimony of it. The human figure of a dominator embodied a divine symbol.

In other words, the Romans were a people deeply committed to their religious beliefs. The concepts of *gravitas* and *dignitas* in Roman culture can serve as an inspiration to all. If the Hyperborean tradition were to be revived, it is conceivable that we might witness the emergence of a leader akin to the Roman emperor during his prime. Such an individual would integrate both political and religious elements into his role, embodying spirituality within his very presence.

Although the forms of the rituals may be new or revised from ancient models, it is imperative that we maintain rituals. Therefore, we should ensure that these traditional yet modern rituals are both elegant and dignified.

CHAPTER SEVEN

REVOLT AGAINST THE MODERN WORLD

R*evolt Against the Modern World* does not advocate for a revolt akin to the French Revolution or any similar modern upheavals. Rather, it emphasizes the need for a conceptual revolution, one that originates from an ancient culture, specifically the Hyperborean. This "polar, northern" cultural strain is believed to have influenced numerous global cultures, including those in China, India, Persia, Egypt, and Rome. Its impact can also be observed in the pagan Nordic-Eddic traditions and Amerindian cultures.

Evola's book is a careful and often detailed critique of the author's view of the modern world. This world is marked by US and Soviet dominance, widespread materialism, a uniform culture of mass democracy, propaganda, and entertainment that disregards the mystical, supernatural, and intangible aspects of existence. Evola contrasts this with the "traditional" world, characterized by the man of Tradition. According to Evola, this individual possesses innate superiority due to his virtues and his capacity to act as an intermediary with the aforementioned intangible realm.

Evola suggests that in earlier times, humanity existed in a state of paradise. Now, we live in "states increasingly conditioned by human, mortal, and contingent elements." [Evola 1995, p. 177]

A key aspect of Evola's criticism is that "Tradition" should not be understood as simple conservatism or a longing for a relatable past. Instead, it involves a broader concept that includes supra-human and supra-individual elements, where the divine realm influences human society. Therefore, "Tradition" should be interpreted from a spiritual-esoteric perspective, focusing on an ideal a-historical or supra-historical era rather than a conditional past reality. Evola refers to this perspective as *metahistorical*. This approach aims to conceptually capture the Hyperborean strain.

Revolt Against the Modern World is structured into two sections: the first, titled "The World of Tradition," and the second, "Genesis and Face of the Modern World."

The initial section provides a conceptual overview of the doctrines and symbols of those ancient civilizations identified by the author as "traditional"—that is, cultures where the principle of *divine kingship* was central to society. In such societies, a priest-king governed under the notions of *dharma* and natural law, promoting a glorified harmony that permeated all aspects of life. Historically, this priest-king archetype was embodied by figures such as the Egyptian pharaoh, the Hindu *dharmarāja*, and the Roman emperor. These civilizations, with foundations predating the Kali Yuga, recognized a vertical, metaphysical dimension to reality, wherein material reality (the "horizontal" dimension) was secondary and subordinate. The caste system played a crucial role within this framework.

In summary, the traditional world was characterized by divine kingship, initiation practices for educating the elite, an appreciation for heroic action and contemplation, which collectively facilitated the establishment of empires such as those in epic India, ancient Egypt, Persia, Rome, and the medieval empire of Frederick II Hohenstaufen.

The second section provides a historical overview based on traditional perspectives. It begins with the Hyperborean era, corresponding to the Sat Yuga of gold and truth, and then explores the subsequent periods of decline through the silver, bronze, and iron ages.

Traditionalism is presented in a Hyperborean, polar context. Evola did not develop this idea entirely on his own; he was influenced by French scholar René Guénon. Guénon suggested that Tradition represents a source of primordial light affecting humanity. This light was considered the essence of a superior culture originating in an earlier golden age referred to as Hyperborea. The region known as "Hyperborea" in Greek is called *Paradesha* (paradise) by the Persians, Śveta-dvīpa by the Hindus, Avalon by the Celts, Midgard by the Germans, and Tula or Thule by the Amerindians. Tradition is described as a series of virtual streams of light from the Primordial State, influencing various parts of the world including China, India, the Middle East, Europe, and America. In all these regions, this influx of light contributed to the development of successive cultures, forming a continuous golden chain (*aurea catena*) that impacted true culture everywhere.

In the specific Evolian variety, this tradition represents an elevated primordial state, referred to as "heaven" or true being (Ger. *Sein*), in contrast to derivative becoming (Ger. *Seiendes*). Evola describes a Hyperborean society that originated in a polar region. This society is characterized by attributes such as light, spirit, glory, dharma, solar exuberance, and sacred ecstasy. In those early days, societal divisions such as priest, warrior, or farmer were not present; it was a unified group, transcending any caste distinctions, referred to as Skt. *ativarna*. The culture focused on divinity rather than humanity itself. It was described as *apauruṣeya*, meaning suprahuman, beyond the human condition, which contrasts with contemporary views often favored by modern intellectuals and thinkers. "The roots of authority ... always had a metaphysical content." [ibid p. 8]

As previously mentioned, the most significant aspect of the Hyperborean tradition was the unification of the roles of priest and king. This sacred king, or *dharmarāja*, held a divine lineage. For example, the pharaohs were believed to descend from Horus, while the Nordic-Germanic princes were considered descendants of Odin.

This king had a solar symbol, known as the *sol invictus*. *Gold* was his representative metal. The use of it was ceremonial and symbolic, rather than commercial, illustrated by the conflict seen between the conquistadors and the Inca ruler Atahualpa. – The priest-king embodied "glory," possessing a charisma of invisible yet tangible power in the form of *vril, hvareno, ka, chi.* He was considered the son of heaven, ruling in accordance with dharma, ensuring justice and harmony in society under divine guidance. It was a culture characterized by strength but also influenced by women; the woman's role included being the royal spouse and anima, without being matriarchal as seen in some southern examples. This is illustrated by the *virile, polar, solar, northern* culture versus the *feminine, southern, lunar* culture. The former is associated with Sanātana dharma, Zoroastrianism, Odinism, and Roman imperiality, while the latter is linked to matriarchy like the Greek Bacchantes and perhaps the Abrahamic tradition. Evola favored the former, which he identified with northern light.

A notable aspect of the Hyperborean vision is the symbol of the polar region. As the "top of the world," the traditional priest-king governs by dharma (*dharmarāja*); he oversees the rotation, the wheel, the chakra – including both the rotating earth and the body's rotating plexi, the chakras. He is *chakravartin,* a universal king, representing "the archetype of the regal function." [p. 16]

He governs Midgard, the mandala, and the polar continent. He is recognized as the lord of peace, lord of justice, and lord of the world. Historically known as Prester John, Melchizedek, Manu, or Menes, this role is currently associated with the Dalai Lama, or possibly Mr. Drunvalo Melchizedek from Sedona, Arizona, USA, born in 1941.

This serves as an adequate summary, although the entirety of the *Rivolta* scenario encompasses a broader context.

As mentioned previously, the concept of a golden age is based on the progression of yugas. However, Evola did not grasp that the sequence of yugas is cyclic in nature. He failed to recognize that they proceed initially in a descending arc followed by an ascending arc. Currently, we are in the ascending phase.

Evola believed that the yugas concluded with Kali Yuga. However, the cycles continue beyond this point. The succession of yugas is not linear but cyclic. Following the descending Satya Yuga, Treta Yuga, and Dvapara Yuga, there is a descending

Kali Yuga. Around the year zero, the ascending arc begins, starting with an ascending Kali Yuga, which concludes around 1899 CE. Subsequently, the ascending Dvapara Yuga commences, followed by the ascending Treta Yuga and the ascending Satya Yuga. This progression signifies a return to an ideal state of existence. "We are starlight, we are golden, we are million year old carbon, and we got to get ourselves back to the garden"...

In the descending arc, conditions progressively deteriorate. Evola observed this phenomenon and incorporated it as a fundamental aspect of his worldview in *Rivolta*. However, he was unaware that the decline ceases upon entering the ascending arc.

It is essential for every reader of Evola to keep this in mind.

Evola suggested that the Kali Yuga would eventually end. He wrote *Ride the Tiger* with the message that the dark forces will eventually lose momentum, leading to a resurgence of traditional values.

He perceived the emergence of a new era, encapsulating its essence in *Ride the Tiger*. *Rivolta*, serving as a necessary conceptual foundation for this, presents significant challenges due to its complexity and lack of appeal. However, as indicated earlier, *Pagan Imperialism* offers a more accessible exposition on the identical subject matter. While *Rivolta* delves deeper into the Hyperborean narrative, it does so in a more detailed and scholarly manner.

CHAPTER EIGHT

THE MYSTERY OF THE GRAIL

One Grail narrative that is particularly well-suited to our era is *Parsifal*, authored by Wolfram von Eschenbach.

Unlike some other Grail myths, such as the one in Malory's *Morte d'Arthur*, the mysterious stone in Parsifal does not simply appear and disappear because the world is unprepared for it. Instead, the hero wins it and becomes the ruler of a new era. He assumes the position of the Grail king and leads humanity back to a traditional rule characterized by certain qualities. He heals the sick king and revitalizes the dry tree.

This marks the advent of a new era unfolding before us. It signifies the King of the World as revealed by Guénon.

Evola himself has treated the Grail in *The Mystery of the Grail*.

Did he, like myself, recognise that Eschenbach's Parsifal serves as a guiding light for the new era?

Initially, it may not be apparent. Evola did not formally recognise that the Kali Yuga has ended and that the Dvāpara Yuga has begun. These yugas occur in cycles and do not simply conclude with the end of the Kali Yuga, as Evola had believed. Nevertheless, it is important to acknowledge that he seemed to have some awareness that a new age would eventually commence. This is evidenced by his work *Ride the Tiger,* which provides thoughtful guidance for persevering in the struggle to witness the advent of a new era characterised by spirituality and introspection, reviving customs, attitudes, and moods rooted in the ancient Hyperborean past.

The Grail is overseen by a select group of custodians known as the grail knights. Evola emphasizes the significance that these custodians are knights, or warriors, rather than priests. This distinction highlights a northern, masculine spirituality associated with the knight, contrasted with the southern, lunar, feminine spirituality often linked to the Christian, priestly tradition that has historically sought to incorporate the Grail myth.

The Grail Knight represents a virtual "aristocrat of the soul," serving as the symbolic figurehead for Evola's entire doctrine and exemplifying his beliefs. This archetype embodies the nascent elite: knowledgeable, accountable, and extensively informed—not just academically, but also deeply immersed in practical traditions.

The Grail knight searches for a circular, rotating island described as a "... polar land that spins around its axis and carries along the world in its rotating motion." [p.34] The polar Midgard, also known as the "second Hyperborea," is a circumpolar continent believed to be where early human development took place. It is considered a mythical land where tradition originally formed, influencing many cultures throughout history. This influence is described as a stream of primordial light that impacted cultures around the world, including Chinese, Hindu, Middle Eastern, European, and American.

The Grail saga describes a mythical land, often depicted as a revolving island. At the end of the Arthurian saga, Arthur, mortally wounded after his last battle, is taken to Avalon to be rejuvenated. Avalon represents Midgard, Thule, and Paradesha. The Grail king in the Parsifal saga is the priest-king of Hyperborea, also known as Prester John, dharmarāja, King of the World, Manu, Menes, and Menw.

The Grail king and his knights watched over the Grail, a significant myth of the high Middle Ages. Eventually, accounts of Grail myths ceased to be written, as noted by Evola in his book. Some aspects of the Grail tradition were embraced by the Knights Templar and Rosicrucians, and even within the German Empire, there was a hope for an ideal king with exceptional qualities to emerge; Frederick

II Hohenstaufen, 1194-1250, was seen as a near example of such a king. Evola discusses these points thoroughly. However, he also notes that after the Middle Ages, European culture became increasingly focused on materialism and nihilism. The Grail myth was replicated in "Amadis novels," which presented various marvels within a narrative framework that lacked meaning, and the chivalric tradition of courtly love, originally a spiritual initiation process, was diluted into mere sentimentality and romance.

Evola's book concludes on a rather somber note, suggesting that the Grail tradition appears to be extinct. He also offers some positive messages. His book aims to revive this tradition in the hearts of the aforementioned "aristocrats of the soul".

This transcends critical academic study and historical research. It serves as a significant indicator, pointing towards the symbol of the Grail, which stands as a beacon in the night and represents a meaningful emblem.

The Grail remains in existence, though it is presently concealed, as Guénon indicated. Evola's conclusion asserts that we still have the potential to be Grail knights, embodying the role of Responsible Men in pursuit of spirituality. Following the guidance of Parsifal and Morte d'Arthur, along with the Grail adventures and heroes like Sir Galahad, provides us with the "means to enter into a dimension of suprahistorical realities and, in this way, to gradually reach the certainty that the invisible and inviolable center, the king who must awake, and the avenging and restorating hero are not mere fancies of a dead and romantic past, but rather the truth of those who, today, alone may legitimately be said to be alive." [p. 175]

CHAPTER NINE

W as Evola a Buddhist?

Not entirely. He did not strictly adhere to "the Noble Eightfold Path" in all its precise requirements. However, he was deeply influenced by the mindful strictness of Buddhism. On the other hand, the devout worshipping of higher deities did not appeal to him. Consequently, he rejected both Christianity and Hinduism. Nonetheless, he drew upon certain aspects of the Hindu tradition, such as the Gītā's warrior code. Hence, it can be stated that Evola exhibited an eclectic approach. In this chapter, we will examine his perspective on Buddhism more closely.

A notable aspect of Buddhism is its emphasis on piety. However, in Evola's interpretation, the elements of piety and compassion for all living beings are less emphasized. He portrays primordial Buddhism as an Āryan warrior doctrine, focusing on self-discipline and the attainment of a higher state of consciousness.

According to Evola, willpower elevates one to the level of the absolute and unconditional. Through *samādhi* – concentrated thought – one gains control over both life and death. Evola's interpretation of primordial Buddhism emphasized these aspects. However, regarding later Buddhism, specifically Mahāyāna, he only recognized Japanese Zen Buddhism.

Evola commended the asceticism found in Buddhism, asserting that Western asceticism had largely diminished by the 20th century. He also critiqued Nietzsche, who was otherwise an inspiration to him, for being formally anti-ascetic. Evola's book on Buddhism, *The Doctrine of Awakening* (1943), underscores this appreciation of Buddhist asceticism. According to Evola, there are two forms of asceticism: active and passive. The former is practiced by stoic warriors, while the latter is embraced by meditating monks. Evola considered Buddhist meditation to be apt for any ascetic disposition, suitable for both contemplative individuals and men of action.

A Higher Level of Consciousness

Evola discussed this topic in *The Doctrine of Awakening – The Attainment of Self-Mastery According to the Earliest Buddhist Texts*. According to Richard Smoley in Parabola 23 (1998), pages 94-96, Julius Evola comprehended the core principles of Buddhism, particularly Theravada Buddhism. He noted that it does not function as a conventional, organized religion, as it lacks the worship of an external deity.

Evola argues that the enlightened adept appears to represent all that individuals typically revere. This is a profound observation. With this perspective, one can comprehend how Buddha ultimately became venerated as a deity.

According to Evola, as cited by Smoley, Buddhism involves disciplining and purifying one's consciousness to attain a higher level of awareness. This is achieved through ascetic practices and meditation. The primary aim is to reach an elevated state of consciousness. Worship of deities and adherence to moral commandments are not considered adequate alternatives.

Smoley expresses concerns regarding Evola's position as a radical rightist and traditionalist, noting that Evola advocates for society to be governed by eternal, transcendent values. Nonetheless, Smoley acknowledges that Evola's perspective on Buddhism is accurate.

Gautama Buddha's family belonged to the kṣatriya class, which was part of the Indo-European ruling elite. Evola sees Gautama's ancestry as crucial for him to arrive at the specific, esoteric truth of his teaching. Smoley disagrees, citing early Buddhist texts like the Dhammapada, which say ancestry, birth, and hairstyle are irrelevant to becoming a priest. "He who has truth and Dharma, the pure is a brahman."

Gautama Buddha, though a kṣatriya prince, imparted esoteric teachings that, similar to the "Āryan" Vedas of Hinduism, built upon an earlier indigenous esoteric tradition. This indicates that focusing on racial aspects in esotericism can be misleading. However, for those who are interested in the Indo-European warrior tradition and seek spiritual growth, the teachings of Buddha may serve as an entry point to explore these concepts further.

Evola's book provides comprehensive insights into Buddhism. It discusses concepts such as reincarnation, which Evola did not personally believe in and asserted was not addressed in the Pāli Canon. It also covers the noble eightfold path, which he did not practice. Additionally, the book explores the idea of freeing oneself through meditation from the mundane reality of everyday life (referred to as "seeing through the veil of maya") and perceiving beyond the dualisms of daily existence, such as "good/evil" and "friend/enemy."

Evola's elucidation of the *niddana chain* has been highly praised, particularly his explanation of how ignorance and unrestrained desires lead to perpetual rebirth and continuous enslavement in samsara. Evola formulated his Buddhist concept based on an

Italian translation of the Pāli Canon, which comprises the foundational texts of Theravada Buddhism and is rooted in the teachings of Gautama Buddha.

A Lifeline

In Evola's autobiography, *Path of Cinnabar*, he describes his first encounter with Buddhism, which played an important role in his spiritual development. After returning from the First World War, Evola found it difficult to resume his previous way of life. Contrary to the intentions of those who initiated the war, his experiences elevated him spiritually. He explored Dadaism and experimented with drugs (both of which he later rejected but acknowledged as part of his journey), eventually discovering esotericism, beginning with Buddhism.

Overall, these were challenging times for him. As mentioned earlier in the study, he ultimately considered suicide. However, a statement by the Buddha in Majjhima Nikaya I,1 influenced him to reconsider his decision.

Buddha says:

> He who takes extinction to be extinction and, having taking extinction to be extinction, thinks of extinction, thinks of extinction, thinks of extinction, thinks 'Mine is extinction', and rejoices in extinction, such a person, I say, does not know extinction. [Buddha after Evola 2009, p. 16]

Evola later understood that the inclination towards self-destruction was a manifestation of ignorance, rather than an expression of genuine freedom. He highlighted this realization in *Path of Cinnabar* [ibid]. Furthermore, in *The Doctrine of Awakening*, he stated that his motivation for writing the book was to express his gratitude for the doctrine that ultimately prevented him from committing suicide.

CHAPTER TEN

MEN AMONG THE RUINS

Strictly speaking, *Men Among the Ruins* is Evola's sole political work. It is his only book dedicated to political thought and theories of government. The discussion framework is rooted in Western thought, referencing notable figures such as Plato, Thomism, and Donoso-Cortès. Unlike his other works, this book does not extensively explore the Hyperborean tradition and its mythic elements, such as solar kings and ancient Olympic events. Instead, Evola focuses on more grounded and relatable aspects of "governmental studies".

This book also incorporates a well-known concept from Evola, such as the notion of the "Absolute Man". This prominent figure is envisioned as governing the polity in a comprehensive and integrated manner. He is the deliberate individual who serves as the foundational element of any political entity. This figure stands as an alternative to the liberal individual, who is inherently atheistic and mechanistic.

What should the ideal state be like? This was the question that Evola addressed in *Men Among the Ruins*, published in 1952. The book outlines Evola's post-war views on statecraft.

He aimed to deliver a political statement that served as both a positive doctrine for individuals in conflict with the chthonic culture of post-war Italy, and indeed all of Europe, as well as a delineation against totalitarian ideologies such as Fascism and Nazism. His objective was to present a more thoughtful theory of the state, rooted in Tradition and positioned against Liberalism, Communism, Fascism, Nazism, and Catholic conservatism. The outcome is quite noteworthy. It offers a comprehensive theory that employs concepts like *the person* and *the organic state* to challenge the sterile rationalism of Liberalism.

Timeless Principles

In chapter one of *Ruins*, the Evolian political theory is founded in ontology. This concept can also be described as "anchoring it in a higher realm." Evola himself calls it a theory with "the chrism of a superior legitimacy," with "principles from above". [Evola 2002, p. 115]

These types of enduring concepts are not influenced by historical events or changes, nor are they subject to *becoming*. Instead, they are rooted in *being*:

the state, imperium, "authority, hierarchy, justice, functional classes"—these elements form the foundation of Evolian political theory.

They represent "the primacy of the political element over the social and economic elements" [ibid]. Politics should govern society and direct the economy, rather than the current tendency where the reverse often occurs.

Traditional concepts possess an archetypal nature, remaining constant amidst the changes of earthly developments. However, the leftist perspective holds that transformation governs all aspects, including the spiritual domain. According to this view, everything is subject to change. Everything is believed to be conditioned and shaped by age and time.

> According to the revolutionary mentality, there are no principles, systems, and norms with values independent from the period in which they have assumed a historical form, on the basis of contingent and very human aspects such as physical, social, economic, and irrational factors. According to the most extreme and up-to-date trajectory of this deviant mind-set, the truly determining factor of every structure, and of what resembles an autonomous value, is the contingency proper to the various forms and development of the means of production, according to its consequences and social repercussions. [p. 117]

In other words, this conditioned perspective must be avoided when aiming for a nuanced understanding of society, grounded in existence.

To begin with a brief ontological overview: on one side, we have *being*, represented by eternal values, archetypes, symbols, *eidoi*, and *der Urmensch*—divine forms that impart structure to everything below through *influxus*. On the other side, there is *becoming*, characterized by an incessant flow of events, chaos, and disorder, with objects moving erratically under the influence of chthonic forces and *Elementarwesen*. In the words of Evola:

> The former [the realm of being] is the truth upheld by the revolutionary conservative, and by any group that, in the political realm, can be properly characterized as part of an authentic 'Right'; the latter [the realm of becoming] is the myth upheld by world subversion, the common background of all its forms, no matter how extreme, moderate, or watered down they may be. [ibid]

It is important to note that when advocating his ideal state, Evola initially attempts to avoid referring to historical examples. Instead, he focuses on the pure ideal and the timeless principles involved. Nevertheless, some historical references are made below; these references originate both from Evola and from my own contributions.

Sovereignty and Authority

The political discourse formally commences in chapter two, concentrating on the concepts of *sovereignty and authority.* The state functions as the sovereign entity, exercising authority. It stands as the ultimate protector of the realm. In times of crisis, such as an attack against the realm, the sovereign may need to set aside all considerations, including the law. However, during periods of peace, the sovereign enacts laws but remains above the law itself. This notion aligns with Carl Schmitt's perspective: the true sovereign is one who holds the power to make exceptions. This principle applies to both totalitarian and democratic states. During World War II, both dictatorships and democracies suspended civil rights when the survival of the state was at stake.

Evola then distinguishes between *the political realm and the sociological realm.* In this framework, the sovereign embodies political power. The state does not represent societal power, which is defined in sociological terms. As Evola states:

> The State is not the expression of 'society'. The basis of sociological positivism, namely the 'social' or 'communal' view of the State, is the index of a regression and naturalistic involution. It contradicts the essence of the true State, inverting every proper relationship; it divests the political dimension of its proper character, original quality, and dignity. The 'anagogical' [from Greek *ana-gogein,* to lead]

end (namely, of a power drawing upward) of
the State is thus completely denied. [p. 124]

The social and communal dimension may have its
attractions, however, in large-scale politics, it is
often quickly overpowered and absorbed. To wield
influence on an international scale, a sufficiently
sizeable body politic is essential. Consequently, there
arises the necessity for a truly political dimension,
embodied in a state founded on authority and
sovereignty. A small, heartwarming commune with
ideals of direct democracy and citizen participation
does not hold authority in the larger context. Its
sovereignty is rapidly consumed by neighboring
states. Countries protected by geographical barriers,
like Switzerland, are exceptions where a social-
communal ideal can be upheld due to relative
safety from foreign invasion. Nonetheless, this is
a geopolitical anomaly with minimal applicability
in general governmental studies. Therefore, Evola's
emphasis on prioritizing the political dimension
over the social one is valid.

The political domain is characterised by values that
emphasise heroism and a rejection of hedonism.
It encompasses individuals committed to fulfilling
their responsibilities for the collective benefit,
pursuing a shared objective that transcends personal
interests, such as

> peaceful living, pure economics, and physical
> wellbeing, pointing to a higher dimension of
> life and a separate order of dignity [ibid].

This statehood is founded on enduring metaphysical concepts; it can guide life by embodying principles that transcend ordinary existence.

This state asserts "itself over the physical life in order to direct it towards ends, actions, or disciplines that the mere physical life cannot explain or justify." [ibid]

Which social unit forms the foundation of this concept? From what did the state evolve? It is suggested that it evolved not from the family, but rather from the *Männerbund,* an initiatic warrior society of men. Before initiation, a man is simply part of the tribe alongside children and women; post-initiation, he is considered reborn. Consequently, men, as a warrior fraternity, assumed the decisive role of wielding power, viewed as a sacred duty. This perspective on political origins is characteristic of Indo-European traditions, although similar warrior societies could also be found in ancient Africa and America.

The state operates under a masculine framework, whereas society (the *demos*) functions within a feminine framework. The male-female duality is intricate, encompassing both historical and mythical contexts. For instance, there are both male and female deities; similarly, there are *male hieratic cults on mountains and female ecstatic cults in forests,* reminiscent of the archaic period in Greece. Furthermore, mythologies exhibit interactions between male and female gods. In analyzing politics from antiquity to the present, it is essential to recognize its male origins as articulated by Evola; that politics, distinct from the social dimension, was established through male associations. This perspective offers significant clarity.

To illustrate his point, Evola makes an interesting leap by bypassing the development of the Roman *Imperium* and proceeding directly to the concept of the kingdom by the grace of God. He viewed the feudal-style king, ruling alongside aristocratic warrior elites, as ideal because it represented a certain elevation above the mere focus on social and economic factors. Subsequently, the intrusion of the *demos* into politics disrupted the notion of the pure State. Additionally, there was "the degeneration and the obfuscation of the pure principle of sovereignty and authority" [ibid].

Evola discusses the role of nationalism as a contributing factor to societal decline. He argues that governance "by the grace of God" is preferable to governance "by the will of the nation." However, one must here note a significant difference between nationalism in countries below the old imperial *limes* (such as France and Italy) and those above it (such as Germany and Sweden). Evola did not fully grasp this distinction.

Western Europe, north of the ancient Roman limes, constitutes the core of the Faustian era, which aligns with the current Piscean age. In contrast, the territories of the former Roman Empire represent the past, specifically the age of Aries. Therefore, nationalism within the heartland of the Faustian era must be viewed as a forward-looking movement. Nationalism in countries such as France and Italy has long been integrated into the mainstream establishment. Historically and presently, their nationalism is often officially part of the revolutionary and anti-traditional consensus. Conversely, in Germanic regions, nationalism in the 21st century retains a subversive nature, serving as a potent tool in opposing the pervasive influence of the global Empire. The concept of nationalism differs significantly between the southern European *Zivilisation* and the northern European *Kultur*.

Furthermore, when critiquing Evola, it is important to recognize the value of public participation in politics. The concept of democracy, in particular, has a distinct advantage: the possibility of feedback. A political system that lacks a feedback mechanism, such as general elections determining which party or coalition should assume governmental responsibilities, faces the risk of stagnation. Therefore, general elections (ideally free from pervasive globalist propaganda) and the governments they establish possess inherent value. This is an aspect that Evola failed to acknowledge.

The Person

Chapter three of *Ruins* presents noteworthy perspectives. This chapter emphasizes the concept of "the person," a conscientious human entity, as a constructive focal point for society. This emphasis is contrasted with "the individual," which is otherwise celebrated by Liberalism.

The primary issue with modernist ideology, according to Evola, is Liberalism. Although the concept is rooted in the Latin term *libertas,* meaning freedom, modern Liberalism does not fundamentally safeguard freedom.

Why? Because it has a flawed conception of man, viewing him as a lifeless container into which a certain amount of "freedom" can be poured, the same amount for everyone, as equality is yet another liberal ideal.

Freedom, equality, and individualism are fundamental principles of Liberalism. However, this ideology often focuses on the individual in a manner that can be seen as atheistic and lacking depth. According to Evola, we should instead consider the term *the person*, which originates from Catholic thought and denotes a unique free human being endowed with reason and free will. This person does not require the state to bestow freedom upon him, as he is inherently free by birth. Similar to Jünger's concept of *the Anarch*, this individual is naturally conscious and in connection with the Absolute. Thus, it can be argued that the person exists prior to society.

With the person in focus, our Italian guide discusses equality. It is suggested that we need "equality before the law" and "equal opportunities" (no privileges). However, taking equality as a conceptual foundation can lead to complications. For example, describing a group of people as "many equals" can be seen as contradictory.

> [M]any beings that are equal, completely equal, would not be many, but one. To uphold the equality of the many is a contradiction in terms, unless we refer to a body of soulless mass-produced objects. [p. 134]

It is inevitable that in human society there will always be some kind of inequality. And, conversely, 100% equality leads to slavery and helotism. Equality is the will to formlessness.

The individual leads to robotic societies governed by "the reign of quantity" (a term borrowed from Guénon), whereas *the person* leads to differentiated societies. Acknowledging "inequality means to transcend quantity and admit quality." [ibid]

An individual is part of the realm of pure matter, specifically the inorganic state. For example, a non-crystallized mineral can be fragmented into smaller parts while maintaining its identity as the same mineral. In contrast, higher-order plants and animals, when divided, either perish or become diminished forms of their original state. These organisms are governed by form-giving forces (*eidoi*) and possess qualities that extend beyond mere material composition. "Therefore, the atomic ... 'free' individual is under the aegis of inorganic matter, and belongs, analogically, to the lowest degrees of reality." [p. 135]

"Equality" is relevant primarily when considering a social aggregate, focusing on the most fundamental aspects of existence. It is universally acknowledged that everyone requires food, sleep, and shelter. Even Evola concurs with this notion; however, he contends that this aspect of human beings is the least compelling. It is like "regarding as paramount the bronze found in many statues, rather than seeing each one as the expression of distinct ideas, to which bronze ... has supplied the working matter." [ibid]

The foundation of any thoughtful political theory is the person. *The person* is a differentiated human being, aware of his intrinsic value, whereas *the individual* is a singular, mechanical entity prone to propaganda and conditioning.

The person is inherently unique, and this uniqueness leads to inherent differences. Promoting this "right to inequality" encourages spiritual growth. On the other hand, pursuing uniform equality within society may result in regression, loss of individuality, and lack of distinctiveness.

Equality

Considering *the person* as the fundamental unit fosters diversity and multiplicity, resulting in hierarchical structures. Some individuals possess greater spiritual aptitude than others, as encapsulated in the classical wisdom: *suum cuique tribuere*, meaning "to each his own." This principle underpins a society of discerning beings, while Kant's categorical imperative, which advocates for the universalization of one's actions, tends towards uniformity and ultimately, servitude. Equality is feasible only among individuals who are equal on a certain level within a hierarchical framework. Among individuals with comparable levels of "personhood," equality can exist. However, imposing a uniform standard of equality for all individuals leads to a mechanistic, ant-like society.

In the same vein, freedom can only be realized in a hierarchical structure: "*[J]ustice* means to attribute to each and every one of these degrees a different right and a different freedom. ... [E]verybody enjoys the freedom he deserves, which is measured by the stature and dignity of his person or by his function, and not by the abstract and elementary fact of merely being a 'human being' or a 'citizen'". [p. 136] Proclaiming universal freedom is a concept often used in revolutionary contexts. Absolute, unconditioned freedom does not exist in any practical sense; all functioning societies have various forms of liberties. Any form of equality naturally sets boundaries on freedom. In discussing freedom, Evola distinguishes between "*to be*" and "*to do*;" having the liberty to do everything you want is impractical, whereas having the freedom to be yourself is achievable in a society of individuals. This notion was already acknowledged by medieval Catholicism.

Evola articulates that he has redefined the "immortal principles" of freedom and equality, represented by the "liberté, égalité" of the French Revolution. The third element in the renowned triad, fraternity ("fraternité"), is considered a sentimental addition to the first two. It is understood that true brotherhood cannot be imposed from above upon discerning, autonomous individuals—on *persons*. Brotherhood is something we acquire by birth, not through any abstract principle.

A Differentiated Society

In ethics and politics, the person is paramount. Man precedes society and the state. Moreover, this person should be regarded as a mindful, discerning, and rational human being, rather than an unthinking, subservient helot. A summary of the Evolian perspective on the state is as follows:

Every society and State is made of people; individual human beings are their primary element. What kind of human beings? Not people as they are conceived by individualism, as atoms or a mass of atoms, but people as persons, as differentiated beings, each one endowed with a different rank, a different freedom, a different right within the social hierarchy based on the values of creating, constructing, obeying, and commanding. With people such as these it is possible to establish the true State, namely an antiliberal, antidemocratic, and organic State. The idea behind such a State is the priority of the person over any abstract social, political, or juridical entity, and not of the person as a neuter, leveled reality, a mere number in the world of quantity and universal suffrage. [p. 139]

The Evolian summation further elaborates on the purpose of society, which is to facilitate spiritual development. In order to achieve this, society must consist of individuals who possess a sense of identity and purpose, rather than aimless and disconnected persons. It should also prioritize differentiation and individuation as guiding principles.

Further details of the ideal society are presented. The concept envisions a pyramidal structure, with an Absolute Man at the apex. Although the pyramid symbol may appear somewhat oppressive, perhaps a circle with the leader at the center could be more appropriate. However, adhering to Evolian traditions, we will proceed with the pyramid symbol for now.

Persons make up the different levels of the pyramid – and "being a person is something that needs to be further differentiated into degrees, functions, and dignities with which, beyond the social and horizontal plane, the properly political world is defined vertically in its bodies, functional classes, corporations, or particular unities, according to a pyramid-like structure, at the top of which one would expect to find people who more or less embody the absolute person." [p. 140]

In a previous chapter, we discussed the concept of "the absolute person." This individual has actualized all his potentialities and become the fullest expression of his being. He radiates vital energy, known in various cultures as *vril, hvareno, chi, prāṇa, odic power,* or *mana.* This life force is sacred and integral to his existence. Such a person contrasts sharply with an unthinking and detached individual who is easily swayed by external influences. The absolute person is deeply rooted in his essence, exercising precise control over his thoughts, emotions, muscles, and nerves. This is what it takes to embody pure authority, "to assume the symbol and the power of sovereignty, or the form from above, namely the *imperium.*" [p. 140]

This is the differentiated model of society, one defined by being rather than mere becoming. This is the Evolian payoff:

> Going from humanity, through 'society' or a collectivity based on natural law and the nation, and then proceeding in the political world all the way to a personality variously integrated, and finally to a dominating super-personality, means to ascend from lower degrees to degrees that are increasingly filled with 'being' and value, each one the natural end of the previous one: this is how we should understand the principle according to which man is the end or the primary end of society, and not vice versa. [ibid]

The concept of "follow the leader" serves as a guiding principle, but it is not about blind obedience. In this context, an esteemed leader elevates his followers, bringing them to his level and inviting them into his circle of influence. This idea can be traced back to Plato, and Julius Evola describes the importance of trusting an inspired leader in this elite school of political thought.

> To depend on such leaders constituted not the subjugation, but rather the elevation of the person; this, however, makes no sense to the defenders of the 'immortal principles' and to the supporters of 'human dignity' because of their obtuseness. It is only the presence of superior individuals that bestows on a multitude of beings and on a system of

disciplines of material life a meaning and a justification they previously lacked. *It is the inferior who needs the superior, and not the other way around.* The inferior never lives a fuller life than when he feels his existence is subsumed in a greater order endowed with a center; then he feels like a man standing before leaders of men, and experiences the pride of serving as a free man in his proper station. The noblest things that human nature has to offer are found in similar situations, and not in the anodyne and shallow climate proper to democratic and social ideologies. [p. 142]

The elite leads society to new glorious heights. Again, we come to the *anagogical* function, mentioned above. The mindful state should lead (Greek *anagogein*) the citizens to reach their full potential.

It is about "arousing and nourishing the individual's disposition to act and to think, to live, to struggle, and eventually to sacrifice himself for something that goes beyond his mere individuality" [p. 143]

This requires leaders who are mindful, possess genuine spiritual objectives, and allow for divine *influxus* at all levels. Without these elements, this anagogical function risks devolving into a dictatorship similar to that seen in the 20th century or into the current form of bland utilitarianism.

Evola implies that this state leads to totalitarianism. Conversely, establishing a society based on mindful individuals ensures protection against a disordered and unthinking mass culture.

In chapter three, Evola presents a critique of contemporary liberal democracy, challenging the principles associated with "1789". While we, for our part, stress certain important tasks (such as the necessity for a political system to have a feedback mechanism, which democracy can provide, and the significance of northern nationalism), we here summarize Evola's argument in accordance with his style. Evola seeks to ground his discussion in concepts that transcend modern political thought:

> To go back to the origins means, plainly and simply, to reject everything that in any domain (whether social, political, or economic) is connected to the 'immortal principles' of 1789, as a libertarian, individualistic, and egalitarian thought, and to oppose it with the hierarchical view, in the context of which alone the notion, value, and freedom of man as *person* are not reduced to mere words or excuses for a work of destruction and subversion. [p. 147]

Organic State Concept

Chapter four of *Ruins* examines the concept of the organic state, consistent with the notion of the person as both terms are comprehensive and integrative. The individual recognizes his inner divine light, possesses free will and rationality, and exists autonomously among other free beings in various roles, such as family member, professional, and citizen. Such a perspective aligns with an *organic concept of the state*, which is reminiscent of the classical ideas found in Plato's *The Republic*.

What is Evola's definition of an organic state? It refers to something living, more than just a collection of parts:

> A state is organic when it has a center, and this center is an idea that shapes the various domains of life in an efficacious way; it is organic when it ignores the division and the autonomization of the particular and when, by virtue of a system of hierarchical participation, every part within its relative autonomy performs its own function and enjoys an intimate connection with the whole. In an organic State we can speak of a 'whole' – namely, something integral and spiritually unitary that articulates and unfolds itself – rather than a sum of elements within an aggregate, characterized by a disorderly clash of interests. [p. 149]

Historically, the organic state has always been governed by a central authority symbolizing sovereignty and power. It was led by responsible individuals who upheld their commitments; the government was not merely a collection of equals engaged in casual discussions, with members avoiding accountability whenever possible. Beneath this ruling figure were various social bodies (such as castes, classes, and councils) that maintained some level of autonomy but were willing to sacrifice a portion of their freedom for the greater good. Even opposition forces could be integrated into the overall structure, similar to the role of the opposition in the classic British parliamentary system (hence the term "His Majesty's loyal opposition"). This organic state functioned like a symphony orchestra under the leadership of an absolute authority; a spiritual essence permeated every part. An influxus of influence from above, potentially from a divine source, ensured this cohesion. While Evola does not explicitly mention "God" or "influxus," his model readily accommodates these concepts.

The organic society has room for instances like "personality, true freedom, daring and responsible initiative, and heroic feats." [p. 151]. This statement succinctly represents the traditionalist ideal. Nihilist establishments oppose values such as individuality, freedom, responsibility, and heroism.

Evola's discussion highlights the distinction between the *ancien régime* glory of the organic state and the totalitarian state. Contrary to popular belief, the alternative to liberal democracy is not limited to Fascism, Nazism, or Bolshevism. Contemporary left-leaning perspectives often overlook these distinctions, as was the case during Evola's time in Italy and remains true in 21st-century Europe. According to Evola, the doctrinal fault of the totalitarian state lies in its imposition of order through materialistic and controlling forces rather than through spiritual influence.

The totalitarian state promotes a cult-like worship of the state, often referred to as "statolatry". For example, Fascism's motto is, "Everything by the state, nothing without the state, nothing against the state," and the Nazi slogan states, "The state is all – you are nothing" (as quoted by Jünger in *Jahre der Okkupation*). This deification and idolization of what is secular starkly contrasts with the functions of an organic state, which are inherently spiritual and oriented towards transcendence. Statolatry represents a modern form of political fetishism, made possible only within a context of materialism.

Taking an Oath

A fundamental aspect of any human society, both historical and contemporary, is the practice of taking oaths. Jünger notably remarked that "you can't swear an oath with atheists," suggesting that the act of swearing an oath inherently assumes the presence of invisible, superior forces that influence our lives. Despite this, the modern state continues to require judges, officials, and members of the armed forces to take oaths. Evola provides a comprehensive critique of the practice of oaths in the modern era:

> This is indeed absurd or even sacrilegious when the State, in one way or another, does

not embody a spiritual principle: an oath
in such a case would be an instance of State
worship. Where the meaning of what an oath
is all about has been completely lost, how can
one be willing or required to swear such an
oath, if the State is nothing more than what
modern 'enlightened' ideologies claim it to
be? A mere secular authority ... as such has no
right to require an oath, no matter what the
circumstances. [p. 153]

In contrast, the function of the oath in traditional
society can be described as follows:

Conversely, we find oaths to be a normal and
legitimate essential element in the political
organization of an organic and traditional
type; an example is found with the oath
of loyalty, which was regarded as a true
sacrament, the *sacramentum fidelitatis,* in the
feudal world. In Christianity, this type of oath
represented the most terrible of all oaths: in
the words of an historian, 'it made martyrs
out of those who gave their lives in order to
remain faithful to it, just as it damned those
who violated it.' [p. 153-154]

Economy

Chapter six of *Ruins* addresses the concept of work.
Work is described as the chthonic-helotic aspect
of human activity, in contrast with the creative

endeavors of artists and artisans, and the activities of inspired leadership in both peace and war – these are considered deeds rather than work. Creativity and deeds are hallmarks of a traditional society; referring to them as "work" reduces individuals to mere proletarians. While work is seen as alienating, handiwork is regarded as fulfilling.

Now, we turn our attention to the topic of economy, which is also discussed in this chapter. As someone aptly stated, "World history teaches us that no people became great through economics; it was economics that brought them to their ruin." Economic value is generated through diligent work and prudent saving, rather than the accumulation of money, usury, or speculative practices.

Today's liberal democracies primarily aim to generate wealth and create prosperity, with economic growth as their main objective. However, Evola suggests that the focus should instead be on achieving *economic independence*, which benefits both individuals and the state. Therefore, striving for freedom from multinational influences is a national goal worth pursuing, even if it results in reduced prosperity. Autonomy, even accompanied by austerity, is preferable to economic dependence on international entities.

Historicism

In chapter seven, Evola critiques the concept of historicism. Historicism, as formulated by Hegel, views history as progressing from primitive and disordered forms to more complex and developed ones, exemplified in German history leading to the establishment of the Prussian Kaiserreich. In contrast, Evola's model sees early history as a golden age of sacred royalty with direct access to being, rather than primitive. Hegel's model is perceived by Evola as another concept for a culture of becoming. To this we like to add, that while Hegel's historical model may have its flaws, the ascendancy of Germany during the Faustian age, starting around 1413 CE, represents a significant period for future development. This period signifies the heartland of the Faustian *Kultur,* succeeding the Greco-Roman *Zivilisation* that includes Europe below the *limes.*

Italy, Evola's native land, is part of a *Zivilisation* proud of its ancient heritage, known for its empire-building and the *Pax Romana.* This period symbolically ended with the sack of Rome in 1527. From then on, European history, and world history, was largely influenced by Western Europe with Germany playing a significant role. However, Evola maintains a vision of future Italian prominence. Therefore, chapter eight of *Ruins*, which discusses aspects of Italian history, may be less compelling to some readers. Never the less, Evola offers a unique perspective by criticizing Italy's city-state period and promoting the Ghibelline ideal of the Hohenstaufen empire. Additionally, he challenges the *Risorgimento* narrative, viewing it as orchestrated by elite secret societies rather than a spontaneous popular revolt. The unification of Italy in the mid-19th century also led to Italian nationalism, although this movement is generally considered less robust compared to the German-Nordic variety, which had more characteristics of a widespread popular movement.

Italy has a rich history. Discussions, such as those in chapter eight by Evola, explore various perspectives on its development.

Italy and the capital of Rome are strong European symbols, loaded with historical and mythical power. However, the future of Europe and the world lies with Faustian empire builders, not southern Europe, which has its empire in the past.

Militarism

Chapter Nine addresses the topics of militarism and military governance.

The subject was briefly mentioned earlier in the book, presenting Evola's critique of historical rule by soldiers, whether manifested through Bonapartism, ancient Greek tyrants, or Renaissance-style *condottieri*. It is important to note that Evola opposes these forms of governance due to their lack of spiritual influence and *influxus*, "lacking any higher consecration" [p. 157].

From a broad perspective on military dictatorships of a totalitarian nature, it is argued that regimentation and the idealization of "the barracks" might result in a rigid, uninspired, and mechanistic society. Even Evola acknowledges this point. Nevertheless, when a nation faces threats from violent leftist forces, a so-called "veto coup" by the military may be necessary, as observed in 20th century Spain, Turkey, and Greece; Evola mentions this in passing. Furthermore, in a traditional sense, the soldier can provide a metaphysical direction for society. The concept of the *Männerbund* is once again upheld as an ideal. In the perennial conflict between Uranian forces of light and order and telluric forces of darkness and chaos, the *Männerbund* soldier can engage in a *bellum justum* (just war) for the common good, culminating in a *pax triumphalis* (triumphant peace).

The Imperium, directed by divine guidance, is founded on the principle of "military might under law." Soldiers, traditionally anchored in their roles, embody the concepts of sacrifice and heroism, which are not commonly found elsewhere in society. This contrasts *rule by the sword* with *rule by the pen*. Governments with military personnel forming the core of civil servants (such as Meiji Japan and the German Kaiserreich) tend to be less susceptible to corruption compared to those predominantly staffed by civilian clerks (such as China and Italy during the same period). These military bureaucrats serve in uniform. Evola's depiction of the Prussian spirit in civil service, extending into the economic sphere, is illustrated as follows:

> The Prussian style did not apply only to the military: by defining itself as 'Frederickianism,' it shaped one of the most austere and aristocratic European military traditions, but also manifested its influence in everything that is service to the State, loyalty, and anti-individualism. This style educated a class of government officials according to principles very different from mere bureaucracy, petty clerical spirit, and the irresponsible and lazy administration of the affairs of the state. Moreover, this style never failed to act in the economic sector, ensuring, at the onset of the industrial era, an intimate cohesion to great industrial complexes led by quasi-dynastic lines of entrepreneurs who were respected and obeyed by the workers almost in terms of military loyalty and solidarity. [p. 197-198]

Modern warfare in the 20th century had the potential to cultivate individuals of exceptional capability. Politics involves struggle, with war representing the most extreme form of political conflict. Heroism is developed within this political realm, rather than in the social context of antimilitarism, where the ideal is "peace at any cost."

Imperium

Chapter ten is about Catholicism versus Ghibellinism, and the church versus imperium. Regarding my personal views on Catholicism, I hold that, politically, the Catholic church needs reformation. Corruption isn't just a historical feature in this case; it is about more than some wayward Renaissance popes. I'd say, Catholicism is politically-symbolically a rule of "men in skirts"; better then, to have Teutonic knights under a man like Frederick Hohenstaufen running the show, a model of justice, responsibility, and spiritual inclination. Evola's depiction of Ghibellinism supports this idea.

> In its deeper aspect, Ghibellinism more or less claimed that through the view of earthly life as discipline, militia, and service, the individual can be led beyond himself and reach the supernatural culmination of human personality through action and under the aegis of the Empire. This was related to the character of a nonnaturalistic but 'providential' institution acknowledged in the Empire; knighthood and the great knightly Orders stood in relation to the Empire in the same way in which the clergy and the ascetic Orders stood in relation to the Church. These Orders were based on an idea that was less political than ethical-spiritual, and partially even ascetic, according to an asceticism that was not cloistered and contemplative, but rather of a warrior type. In this last regard, the

> most typical example was constituted by the Order of Knights Templar, and in part by the Order of the Teutonic Knights. [p. 207]

The Roman emperor held the title of *pontifex maximus*, meaning "builder of bridges," acting as a mediator between heaven and earth. The Ghibelline emperor followed this ideal. The popes later adopted the *pontifex maximus* title, which originally represented the Hyperborean tradition of *vita activa* priest-kings, rather than the *vita contemplativa* nature associated with the popes.

In summary, this represents the concept of "Ghibellinism" as interpreted by Evola.

In my professional opinion, the future is entrusted to a leader with exceptional spiritual insight.

To specifically call this "Ghibellinism," though, is a moot point.

"Ghibellinism" is part of the Evolian jargon and not a useful term today.

The Rest

In the subsequent chapters of *Ruins*, the content may be of lesser interest. However, chapter thirteen, which addresses "occult war," including secret history and conspiracies, offers valuable insights.

The exploration of elite club influence in early modern and modern European history is crucial, as it is seldom covered by other notable political theorists. While historians such as Nesta Webster have made significant contributions in this area, further examination is warranted. Essentially, elite clubs played a pivotal role in directing the French Revolution, the revolution of 1848, the Paris Commune, and the Russian Revolution of 1917. This chapter provides a conceptual overview of these events, which we will not elaborate on here, having already discussed them to some extent in *Actionism* (2017).

Chapter fourteen delves into the Roman soul and the Latin character, presenting an engaging topic from a cultural perspective. Politically, it contrasts Italy's historical context with Germany's future, as previously mentioned. The Roman ideal, as articulated by Evola, is thoroughly examined in *Pagan Imperialism* (referenced earlier). The following Roman ideals remain pertinent in Italy: *virtus* (denoting virile spirit and courage rather than moralism), *fortitude* and *constantia* (spiritual strength), *fides* (loyalty), and *gravitas* and *solemnitas* (a measured and moderate seriousness).

Lastly, we have *religio* and *pietas,* "which do not mean 'religiosity' in the Christian sense of the word, but instead signify for a Roman an attitude of respectful and dignified veneration for the gods and, at the same time, of trust and reconnection with the supernatural, which was experienced as omnipresent and effective in terms of individual, collective, and historical forces." [p. 259]

Chapter sixteen of *Ruins* examines the idea of a united Europe. Evola suggests that a united Europe, grounded in traditions, is important. He contrasts this with his perspective on the current European Union, which he describes as focused on merchant interests, and a divided "Europe of regions," which he views as lacking central authority.

In my opinion, such a "Balkanized" Europe, sometimes lauded by today's right-wingers, will be easy prey for a resurgent Russia. Russia might not simply take it – but – it will exert *hegemony* over it, like it virtually did during the Cold War. Russia from the east, and the US from the west, could easily become the masters of a weak and divided Europe. Thus, some unity must be created in this part of the world.

Coda

This concludes our summary of *Men Among the Ruins*. As previously noted, it exemplifies Evola's "transparent" style, where he addresses more accessible topics such as statecraft, political science, and various forms of government. For those interested in Evola's work but who prefer to avoid explicit mysticism and esotericism, this study is a valuable resource.

CHAPTER ELEVEN

RIDE THE TIGER

It is possible that he mellowed over the years. The post-WWII Evola may have been different from the preacher of the 1930s. Towards the end of his life, Evola might have revised some of his beliefs. He dismantled his metanarratives, reduced his ambitions, and reinterpreted parts of his previous statements.

He may not have explicitly retracted any conceptual statements he made. However, an examination of the work *Ride the Tiger* reveals a shift from "grand, universal, one-size-fits-all" perspectives to focusing on "the person," the meditating *jīvātman* as the foundation of all things.

Evola's seminal works, *Revolt Against the Modern World* (1934) and *Men Among the Ruins* (1953), present his belief in a return to antiquity. He posits that the grandeur of the Roman Empire, with its stoic warriors and profound religious sentiment, represents an enduring ideal. In response, it is acknowledged that the spirit of the Roman Empire was indeed impressive. Republican Rome exhibited an all-encompassing worldview and approach to life, which have since diminished. The society was inherently religious, stoic, and genuine. During that era, individuals did not select a particular life philosophy; instead, they were integral components of a larger entity where the esoteric creed was inherently present.

In his adherence to traditional Roman ideals, Evola posited that it would be beneficial to reconstruct and emulate the principles of ancient Roman life, essentially advocating for a return to living as if we were Romans today.

However, that approach is unlikely to be successful.

Jumping over your own shadow is impossible; it defies nature's laws.

In the 20th century, Mussolini's Italy was unable to achieve its imperial ambitions. Evola contributed to its metapolitical ideas. However, he did not fully endorse the regime. He believed that it was necessary to embrace the ancient spirit in its entirety, rather than accepting a modified romantic and derivative version.

Over time, Italian fascists grew weary of Evola's antiquated beliefs. However, Evola continued to uphold the ancient, "total" ideal of society even into the 1950s. His work, *Men Among the Ruins* (1952), aims to present an ideology that encompasses society in a manner reminiscent of ancient Roman traditions, advocating for their revival.

It is possible to retain Roman ideals with necessary modifications. However, when developing a new creed for the post-World War II society, it is important to momentarily set aside societal concerns and concentrate on the individual, specifically the person, the mindful individual with the potential to become Absolute Man. This forms the foundation. Evola, after authoring *Men Among the Ruins*, perhaps recognized that it is not feasible to fully restore Tradition in the present, challenging era, at least not on a societal scale. Consequently, his subsequent book focused on the options available to individuals within this context of pervasive materialism.

This conceptual perspective is presented in one of Evola's later works, *Ride the Tiger* from 1961. Comparing *Ride the Tiger* with *Men Among the Ruins* may seem overly simplistic, yet it is worth noting that *Ruins* addresses Tradition at a societal level, whereas *Ride the Tiger* explores Tradition on a personal level. While *Ride the Tiger* provides practical insights for individuals amidst the prevalent materialistic chaos, *Men Among the Ruins* feels more like a theoretical discourse. *Ride the Tiger* offers valuable guidance for traditionally-minded individuals navigating today's complex world. Its focus on the individual's actions aligns well with contemporary concerns, underscoring the notion that in this phase of the *Astral War*, "Everything Starts With You" (ESWY), an aphorism from my philosophical framework, *Actionism*.

Ride the Tiger is seen by some as a late period work, reflecting a departure from many of the ideas Evola supported throughout his life. However, others consider this work significant for those interested in traditionalism. It offered guidance to individuals of the post-war era, the Cold War generation, and those seeking alternatives to "turbo liberalism" and hedonism. The book laid out foundational concepts for a future-focused traditionalism.

The view I personally hold on this subject is that modernism has significantly eroded traditional values. Jünger, in his 1932 work *Der Arbeiter*, illustrates how "The World of the Worker" has transformed the earth into an industrial landscape. Evola proposes that rather than lamenting this transformation, one should embrace it, fully engage with modern life, and strategically respond to its challenges. Although he does not explicitly use the analogy of judo, where one uses the opponent's force against him, it is a fitting metaphor for his approach.

Unlike many other conservative intellectuals, he courageously addressed the issues directly.

Literally, he dared to ride the tiger.

It can be considered extreme to delve into pure materialism for spiritual enrichment, as Evola suggests. This attitude has its roots in the Tantra he promoted during the interwar period. Furthermore, it is challenging today to live as a hermit who rejects worldly life, even if one chooses to go to a monastery or join a religious community like Hare Krishna. While organizations such as ISKCON and Christian esotericism have their merits, traditional quietism may seem unconventional in the modern context. It may be more practical to engage actively with society and embrace various experiences. This approach aligns more closely with contemporary values compared to adopting a reactionary stance that rejects many aspects of modern life.

It is certainly possible to live as a hermit and spiritual seeker even in our era. However, completely renouncing the world is difficult, if not impossible. Today, everything is intertwined with politics. Consequently, one must accept this reality and reasonably engage with politics, economics, and global events. While one may retreat to a personal sanctuary between engagements—where quiet reflection, appreciation of art, reading, and writing can remain central to an intellectual's life—the influence of the outside world is far more pervasive than in antiquity. Escaping the modern zeitgeist is unfeasible. The book *Ride the Tiger* encapsulates this essential lesson and proposes an alternative—a form of *affirmative radicalism*—that transcends materialism and nihilism. It offers a response to the irony and dandyism that cultural fatigue often leaves as the sole viable stance for thoughtful individuals.

Evola combines esotericism with traditionalism, Nietzscheanism, and a focused approach. This is neither a strict adherence to commandments nor an unrestrained vitalism, nor simply a devotion to action and power. It involves exercising control over oneself, navigating modern society with its consumerism and propaganda. Evola acknowledges the current state of affairs and, with a disciplined perspective, evaluates the situation and proposes a course of action for contemporary times.

This plan is focused on the individual rather than society. Traditional and modern societal norms, including conventional religion and materialism, are not considered. The approach begins with the individual as the starting point.

The true challenge lies within oneself. Attaining tranquility amidst chaos is crucial. This state of calmness can be achieved through introspection and esoteric practices. It is essential to focus inwardly, even briefly, and draw strength from concealed inner resources. Maintain impeccability, practice controlled breathing, and engage in meditation.

While Evola may have been influenced by Nietzsche, he did not share Nietzsche's belief that God was dead or that all forms of traditional spirituality should be abandoned. Nietzsche held anti-spiritual views, whereas Evola did not. Evola perceived reality in the invisible rather than in the Western world's modern focus on the external world. Grounded in esoteric knowledge and traditional cultural heritage, Evola believed one could engage with the world and counteract its prevailing forces.

This appears to be the late Evola's belief: to live with strength in the present, using tradition as a guiding principle.

It can be stated that the young Evola possessed an artistic sensibility. His essays often exhibited a poignant style.

However, his writing style often exhibited a tendency towards dry intellectualism.

As previously mentioned, *Pagan Imperialism* represents Evola at his stylistic peak within its initial ten to twenty pages. It offers a sharp political and philosophical discourse.

He never reached that height again.

However, in *Ride the Tiger*, he achieves a certain poignance, particularly in the first half of the work.

Let us examine the symbolic imagery of *Ride the Tiger*, specifically the depiction of riding on the tiger's back. This represents the notion that when confronted by the formidable beast of materialism, one should not merely flee. Instead, similar to the "bull jump" in Mycenaean Crete, one should endeavor to mount the back of the attacking animal. As articulated by Evola:

> The phrase chosen as the title of this book, 'ride the tiger'. (...) is a Far Eastern saying, expressing the idea that if one succeeds in riding the tiger, not only does one avoid having it leap on one, but if one can keep one's seat and not fall off, one may eventually get the better of it. [Evola 1961, p 8]

The philosophical implications of this situation—especially for a mindful individual during the turbulent close of a Kali Yuga—are profound. Beyond its significance, it also serves as an exemplary display of stylistic excellence.

> When a cycle of civilization is reaching its end, it is difficult to achieve anything by resisting it and directly opposing the forces in motion. The current is too strong; one would be overwhelmed. The essential thing is not to let oneself be impressed by the omnipotence and the apparent triumph of the forces of the epoch. These forces, devoid of connection with any higher principle, are in fact on a short chain. One should not become fixated on the present and on the things at hand, but keep in view the conditions that may come about in the future. Thus the principle to follow could be that of letting the forces and processes of this epoch take their own course,

while keeping oneself firm and ready to intervene when "the tiger, which can not leap on the person riding it, is tired of running." [ibid]

CHAPTER TWELVE

Evola often addresses straightforward points. He occasionally simplifies complex academic language and clarifies evident ideas.

A prime example of this might be his perspective on modern sports conducted in mountainous regions.

The argument suggests that downhill skiing represents a materialistic form of mountain sport. It relies on mechanical assistance to transport the skier to the summit, allowing him to descend gracefully with the help of gravity. This is applicable regardless of whether the ascent is achieved via a lift to a prepared piste or by helicopter to an isolated area of fresh powder snow.

In contrast, consider the disciplined sport of mountain climbing. In this activity, the climber utilizes his own physical strength to ascend. The vertical ascent, overcoming the force of gravity, is fundamental to the sport.

To distill Evola's concept, he contrasts downhill skiing and mountaineering. He perceives downhill skiing as a communal and materialistic activity, involving queueing and dining in cafeterias. Conversely, he views mountaineering as focused on small groups and individual accomplishments.

This is one of the aspects of *Meditations on the Peaks*, a collection of essays on mountaineering and its mindful qualities. In the example just given, Evola acknowledges that skiing isn't entirely without merit. He himself would sometimes engage in downhill skiing. However, in comparison to mountaineering, skiing was considered part of modern activities. Mountaineering, on the other hand, was associated with traditional practices and an inner awakening. It was viewed as an activity where one exists in the present moment and focuses away from modern comforts and obsessions.

The mountain climber battles nature and the elements, becoming one with the wind, the mountain, and the snow.

In *Meditations on the Peaks*, we learn more about these subjects. Julius Evola was an accomplished mountain climber, having scaled various sites in the Alps. His final wish was to have his ashes entombed within a remote glacier on the Monte Rosa massif in northern Italy. Thus, he metaphorically "disappeared" into the lofty realm of ice and snow, with his essence eternally present as a gentle breeze among the mountain peaks.

This is Actionism. It represents *Action as Being* and *Movement as a State of Mind*. It is a deliberate approach to activity that balances the contemplative life (*vita contemplativa*) with the active life (*vita activa*). It does not compel one to choose between being an elevated, serene recluse or an unthinking "action figure" of modern times. Instead, it harmoniously unites both aspects in the persona of a mountain climber, who through his practice "awakens a deeper interiority." By engaging with the world (or perhaps ascending above it), he cultivates greater mindfulness and awareness of his internal life, inner being, and inner resources. As Evola states: "The inner victory against the deepest forces that surface in one's consciousness during times of tension and mortal danger is a triumph in an external sense, but it is also the sign of a victory of the spirit against itself and of an inner transfiguration." [Evola 1998, p. 4]

High Life

Ascending the mountain symbolizes approaching the divine, akin to Moses receiving the Tables of the Law on Mount Sinai during his time in the desert.

Consider ancient Greece with its renowned mountains, such as Olympus, Ida, and Parnassus.

The Grail saga centers around the Gralsburg, located on Montsalvat—the "mountain of salvation". In Hindu tradition, the sacred mountains are Mount Meru and Mount Kailash. Additionally, German folklore tells of Frederick Barbarossa, a "once and future" savior, who rests in Kyffhäuserberg.

Ascending a mountain causes the surrounding landscape to appear level, transforming everything into a horizon. The entire world, encompassing all human territories, becomes horizontal. Meanwhile, on the mountain, everything turns vertical, oriented towards higher realms.

Friedrich Nietzsche, a prominent philosopher known for his concept of the "Übermensch" or "superman," received many of his transformative insights while residing in the Swiss Alps. An important quotation from Nietzsche, as cited in the current book on page 53, is: "Many meters above sea level, but many more above what is human."

The mountain terrain profoundly inspires a sense of the divine within us. This aligns with Evola's emphasis on transcending the human condition, which is central to his doctrine.

One can compare him with his German contemporary, Ernst Jünger, who also espoused radical conservative views and resisted modernity. Jünger, in his work, introduced the figure of the Forest Walker (German: *Der Waldgänger*), conceptualized in his essay *The Forest Passage*. This figure symbolized an alternative way of living in the modern era, representing discreet protest against the mechanized society, the homogenization, and the pervasive nihilism of contemporary megacities. While the specifics may vary, this modern-day forest dweller is somewhat more approachable compared to the mountain climber.

In his post-World War II writings, Jünger emphasized gardening, entomology, and Bible reading as ideals, presenting a lifestyle that resonated with the average individual. In contrast, Evola maintained a more aloof and elitist stance. The image of standing alone on the mountain as a mountaineer, facing the elements, aptly captures Evola's attitude.

The Eastern Lyskamm

In *Meditations on the Peaks*, the reader is presented with both a philosophical and religious discourse on mountain dwelling, alongside accounts of actual excursions into mountainous regions. During the 1930s, Evola undertook climbs of several challenging summits in Italy and its vicinity. The book includes reprints of various accounts of these expeditions.

He successfully ascended the northern face of the eastern Lyskamm, a mountain located on the border between Italy and Switzerland. This achievement was regarded as noteworthy. The text entitled "The

Northern Wall of Eastern Lyskamm" concludes with the climber's return to the base camp.

> Two hours later we reach the mountain refuge, Gnifetti. We had left there, for our return, two very different and yet complimentary things, a bottle of White Horse whiskey and a text of warrior ascetism, the *Bhagavadgita*. [Evola 1998, p. 53]

The Meaning of Mountaineering

Meditations on the Peaks: Mountain Climbing as Metaphor for the Spiritual Quest was published posthumously, compiling Julius Evola's writings on the metaphysical significance of mountain climbing. In his memoir, *The Path of Cinnabar*, Evola notes that he engaged in high-altitude mountain climbing to elevate his mental state.

In *Actionism* I wrote the following about *Meditation on the Peaks:*

> According to Evola mountaineering combines heroic action with that of reflection and contemplation. Among others he cites what Indian Buddhists have written about living on the heights and meditating. The book also delves into mythology (as in the mountain as an abode of the gods, and the hero who has to climb up the mountain to perform his deed). Even ontologically mountains are important in that they are higher than the

everyday world, being "closer to heaven". Although this analogy is a bit dated it still has its bearing. – Evola lastly mentions the Russian artist Nicholas Roerich who painted strikingly simple, but not simplistic, pictures of mountains and hermits. The colors purple, white and gold were prominent in his paintings, the most spiritual of colors. [Svensson 2017, p. 119]

In *Actionism* I also said this about the spiritual side of mountaineering:

> *Meditations on the Peaks* ... talks about the inner victory. Everything is decided within; this every esotericist knows. But your inner world can also have dangers in store for you. So you have to govern your thoughts and feelings with willpower. This is the inner victory, to defeat your inner demons. The spirit triumphs over itself, transforming itself in the process. That's why both the heroes and initiates of antiquity were surrounded by an aura of sacredness. To be a hero was to have a touch of immortality. – You have to fathom spirituality, live it and incorporate it. Having done this (1) the spirit lives with a natural sense of superiority (2) somatically this is expressed in a noble appearance. True nobility carries with it a sense of elevation, of lightness, of other-worldlyness. [ibid p. 121]

Here are two quotes from Evola's book to provide an understanding of its content and message. The first is from the foreword, where Evola discusses testing oneself as a means of spiritual enlightenment:

> Feeling left with only one's own resources, without help in a hopeless situation, clothed only in one's strength or weakness, with no one to rely upon other than one's self; to climb from rock to rock, from hold to hold, inexorably, for hours and hours; with the feeling of the height and of imminent danger all around; and finally, after the harsh test of calling upon all one's self-discipline, the feeling of an indescribable liberation, of a solar solitude and of silence; the end of the struggle, the subjugation of fears, and the revelation of a limitless horizon, for miles and miles, while everything else lies down below – in all of this one can truly find the real possibility of purification, of awakening, of the rebirth of something transcendent. [Evola 1998, p. 6]

Finally, we will provide a quote from Milarepa, a Buddhist, who praised Being after surviving on a wintry mountain through meditation. This is from chapter four, titled "A Mystic in the Tibetan Mountains":

> Is my spirit really awake? When I look up to the blue sky, the emptiness of what exists is clearly evident to me and I do not fear the doctrine of the reality of things. – When I look at the sun and the moon, enlightenment arises in a distinct manner within my consciousness and I do not fear

spiritual dullness and torpor. – When I look to the mountain peaks, the immutable object of contemplation is clearly perceived by my consciousness and I do not fear the unceasing changes of mere theories. When I look down to the river below, the idea of continuity clearly arises in my consciousness, thus I do not fear unforeseeable events. – When I see the rainbow, the emptiness of phenomena is experienced in the most central part of my inner being and I fear neither that which endures, nor that which passes away. – When I see the image of the moon reflected by the water, self-liberation, freed from all concerns, clearly appears to my consciousness and I do not fear stupidity and frivolity. [ibid p. 28-29]

CHAPTER THIRTEEN

Julius Evola's *Metaphysics of War* presents a distinctive perspective. It is a European document discussing the concept of *kṣatriya dharma*. A similar doctrine can be found in Japanese texts like Hagakure. The book addresses themes such as active nihilism and active ecstasy, emphasizing the role of the warrior.

The book is compiled after Evola's death but it nevertheless presents a fine traditional perspective on war and the warrior, unique in Western literature. Here, "the knight in shining armour" gets his own Hagakure, so to speak. Evola outlines the distinct nature of the warrior according to his analysis in *Rivolta*, which describes a primordial state where noble and responsible rulers consider war as an "ultima ratio regnum," followed by a period where war becomes an end in itself. The former represents the golden age ideal, while the latter symbolizes the iron age ideal.

Battle as an Inner Experience

It is essential for everyone to aspire to higher spiritual levels, irrespective of their role. Even a warrior should not engage in battle solely for conquest or material gain but must instead uphold and fight for principles.

A fundamental principle is to defend one's country, ensuring the protection and survival of its people. Nevertheless, it is important to recognize that maintaining motivation may require a deeper and more nuanced approach. Defending one's country involves not only safeguarding physical territory but also upholding principles of justice and truth, and striving for personal spiritual growth.

A doctrine of this nature is essential to maintain the spiritual well-being of a warrior, even after the conflict has concluded.

Evola examines these ideas in *Metaphysics of War – Battle, Victory and Death in the World of Tradition,* a collection of his essays on war, published by Arktos in the early 2010s. The author uses the four-caste system of ancient India to highlight the significance of viewing war from the perspectives of priests and warriors rather than that of the bourgeoisie and workers. However, the latter perspective became dominant in the West during the 20th century, turning warfare into a form of labor. This shift was also observed by Ernst Jünger, among others.

This topic deserves further exploration. For example, the line from Paul McCartney's "Pipes of Peace," stating, "got to give them all we can 'til the war is won, then will the work be done," reflects the rhetoric of world wars being perceived as labor. The world wars were conducted by capitalist nations (West) and secular states (East). Engaging in such conflicts without awareness may result in becoming cannon fodder; however, understanding the nature of battle and death can lead to spiritual growth. Ernst Jünger emphasized this notion, identifying the esoteric dimension of battle, as highlighted in his work *Der Kampf als Inneres Erlebnis* (*The Battle as Inner Experience*). Although the prevailing zeitgeist might oppose such spiritual elevation, it remains possible to conduct a war with the principles of a kṣatriya, even amidst the material conflicts of the 20th century and the mercenary engagements of the 21st century. This concept extends beyond soldiers; civilians too may benefit from a profound understanding of ontology to navigate life's challenges. Even a student of history can gain valuable insights from Evola's analysis of war and its spiritual implications.

Regardless of the motivation for studying war, it is essential to adopt an ontological perspective. As soldiers, it is crucial to confront the reality of death and objectively assess the nature of battle and war. In contrast, bourgeois idealism—characterized by exaggerated rhetoric that vilifies the enemy while glorifying one's own side—ultimately results in disillusionment and psychological distress among soldiers. Authors such as Rémarque and Hassel have depicted this phenomenon, where individuals are driven solely by a primal fear of death and an instinctive will to survive, losing touch with their humanity. This often leads to a state of lethargy and catatonia.

Hassel's passage in this context requires summarization. It originates from his debut novel, *The Legion of the Damned*, published in 1953. The narrator returns to the Eastern Front after a hospital stay and notices a significant change: his comrades appear strangely absent or as if they are dead. They have lost all hope of surviving and view their lives as utterly hopeless: *They had given up all hope of getting home alive. They considered everything, even their lives, to be hopeless.*

They are in a state of extreme detachment, existing beyond typical human experiences, driven by basic instincts. Evola, in his book, citing a similar passage in Remarque's WWI novel, describes this state as follows: "[A]ll that impels them [the front soldiers] forward throughout the most terrible tests are elemental forces, impulses, instincts, and reactions, in which there is not much human remaining, and which do not know any moment of light." [Evola p. 26]

This situation may arise if an individual possesses a simplistic worldview as a warrior or engages in conflict with an overly superficial belief system.

What's the solution? How to avoid becoming a zombie in the combat zone?

A soldier like Jünger, who regarded the enemy as equals and was not influenced by false idealism or Wilhelminian propaganda, may have coped with the existential trials of war more effectively. By internalizing the battle, he elevated his consciousness to a higher level. Although the success or failure of the overall war objectives remained significant, there was an additional goal: to achieve spiritual growth from the war experience. The ontological nature of the battle itself served as a source of spiritual energy.

Devotio

Jünger discovered this concept more or less autonomously, guided by his own volition and vision. Although he had read *Orlando Furioso*, he had not delved into doctrinal texts such as the *Hagakure* or the *Bhagavad-Gītā*. Additionally, he was likely unfamiliar with the Roman Empire's rite of *devotio*, in which individuals sacrificed themselves to a deity before battle to fight unburdened by thoughts of survival. This practice is described as: "a mysterious unleashing of forces determined by the deliberate sacrifice of [one's] own person, combined with the will not to come out of the fray alive" [Evola p. 122]. Such a *devotio* represented an ontological release that elevated a warrior's consciousness. An instance of this ritual was performed by a Roman general during the battles for Saguntum in 219 BCE, part of the initial Spanish operations of the First Punic War. The contemporary name for the city remains Sagunto, situated on the Spanish Mediterranean coast.

Devotio was conducted through a formal rite involving a proclamation of self-sacrifice to the gods. This act elevated one to a higher level, beyond ordinary existence. I would contend that Jünger achieved this state of determination and excellence in combat intuitively.

Evola, who served as an artilleryman in World War I, shares his extensive knowledge on warrior philosophy influenced by Rome, India, Persia, and the Crusades. In "The Metaphysics of War" (1935) and "The Āryan Doctrine of Combat and Victory" (1941), he examines the Bhagavad-Gītā, discussing how a warrior, committed to dharma, must fight selflessly. The warrior either dies with a clear mind or wins to rule as a peace-seeking leader (BhG 2.37).

> *hato vā prāpsyasi svargaṃ jitvā vā bhokṣyase mahīm*
> *tasmād uttiṣṭha kaunteya yuddhāya kṛta-niścayaḥ*

In the Gītā, it is noted that a warrior should remain indifferent to both fortune and misfortune, as well as victory and defeat. Death is described as merely a transition to another state. The text advises to fight without concern for the outcome and to practice *apatheia* on the battlefield. This concept of equanimity is stated in verse 2.38:

> *sukha-duḥkhe same kṛtvā lābhālābhau*
> *jayājayau*
> *tato yuddhāya yujyasva naivaṃ pāpam*
> *avāpsyasi*

This state of apatheia represents true godliness, not only for warriors but also for ordinary individuals. Additionally, it may evoke thoughts of Carlos Castaneda's teachings. In his esoteric doctrine, the primary figure is the warrior; an adept in sorcery must possess the mindset of a warrior.

> A man goes to knowledge as he goes to war – wide awake, with fear, with respect, and with absolute determination of purpose. [Castaneda 1990, p. 52]

Modern Stoicism

One must approach war with full awareness, a measure of fear, humility, and steadfast determination. This mindset is also examined by Evola in his book. War can be seen as a metaphysical concept, just as metaphysics can be viewed through the lens of warfare; both require the same level of determination and composure. As Goethe remarked, "Everything is decided within."

Evola also recognized this concept. He observed in the Bhagavad-Gītā and other texts the intrinsic nature of a soldier's psyche: it all begins with the individual. The metaphysics of war must be rooted in the personal experiences of the individual. Simply providing soldiers with a superficial ideology such as "die for the king/leader/democracy" will not suffice. While such doctrines may lead to political victory, the metaphysically grounded individual requires a more profound doctrine.

Evola consistently demonstrated a person-focused approach in his writings. He valued the stoicism of the Roman Empire and believed that Rome should be restored with a community spirit permeating society. This belief was a central aspect of Evola's ideology during the interwar period. However, after World War II, he adjusted his stance and adopted a more reflective position.

With his focus on esoteric thought and a foundation in spirituality, Evola continued to advocate for heroism based on personal qualities rather than state allegiance, even after the war. In the final essay of *Metaphysics of War*, published in 1950 and titled "The Decline of Heroism", he argued for the necessity of ideal heroism. He posited that it is impossible to defend mass society when consumerism, nihilism, and pacifism are predominant ideals. One cannot effectively engage in conflict driven by visions of security and abundance; instead, one must clear one's mind, remain sober and realistic, yet be resolutely prepared to face challenges head-on.

This represents the core of Evola's post-war philosophy: how to confront contemporary challenges with sobriety, engage in global political dynamics, and simultaneously derive individual benefit. One must maintain composure amidst turmoil, akin to the calm centre of a tornado where tranquility prevails despite the surrounding chaos. By cultivating inner peace, one can exert influence on one's environment, especially during turbulent times. The notion is to leverage conflicts for personal strength, acknowledging their presence without ignoring them. This mindset is exemplified by the character Aeon Flux, as highlighted by Trevor Goodchild's perturbing inquiries:

> "You're skating the edge…"
> "I *am* the edge."
> "You're out of control."
> "I take control."
> "What do you really want"
> "You can't give it, you can't take it, and you JUST DON'T GET IT…!"

Rising Mentally or Perishing

Evola demonstrates considerable insight. In his current work, "The Decline of Heroism," he references Jünger, as mentioned earlier. The Italian scholar commends how the German author depicts the modern *material war* (*Materialkrieg*), characterised by attrition warfare with extensive artillery use, which compels individuals to either mentally elevate themselves or succumb. One must attain the absolute and draw strength from its source to overcome internal struggles.

The *Metaphysics of War* presents a series of relatively accessible essays that delve into the metaphysical aspects of war, addressing the intrinsic characteristics of battle. These insights are valuable not only for those in conflict but also for civilians during peacetime. It emphasizes the universal challenge we face: to confront our struggles and elevate ourselves spiritually to withstand the challenges of daily life. Engaging in social life requires more than simply drifting along; it demands clarity of purpose and the ability to navigate challenges with determination. Achieving this necessitates tapping into inner, often concealed, spiritual resources. This, in essence, encapsulates the core message of the metaphysics of war.

CHAPTER FOURTEEN

Under the heading "The Mindful Evola," we will examine various elements of Evolian philosophy, incorporating both Hindu principles and my own philosophical approach, Actionism.

Evola once wrote a review of Guénon's *Man and His Becoming According to the Vedānta (L'homme et son devenir selon le Vedānta,* 1925).

This text by Evola is titled "A Controversy About the Vedānta". It discusses the ancient Hindu school of Vedānta, which is a philosophy focused on renouncing the world and pursuing union with the godhead. It deals with the concept of an impersonal God as the supreme source of reality. According to this philosophy, the individual soul originates from the eternal divine light, and for humans, recognizing their connection with this source is considered the highest good. The phrase *Tat tvam asi* translates to "this eternal Brahman, it is you."

Guénon advocated a creed and moral values anchored in metaphysical reality. In contrast, Evola, who was a magician, did not support this perspective. He viewed everyday reality as power, while Guénon, following Vedāntic principles, considered it an illusion. Evola did not adopt a quietistic approach by turning away from the world; instead, he engaged with it actively, aiming to shape and dominate it. This aligns with Evola's "yoga of power," which can be described as a form of Actionism influenced by Tantric elements.

Evola could be described as a modern Faustian visionary. In his review of Guénon's *Man and His Becoming According to the Vedānta*, he states: "In fact the western spirit is specifically characterized by free initiative, assertion, the value of individuality, a tragic conception of life, and a will to power and action." Within this context, Evola found Vedānta to be somewhat too passive and complacent for his tastes.

As previously mentioned, Evola opposed the Vedāntist inclination to perceive everything as an illusion. To those who claimed "nothing is real," he could theoretically respond: "You assert that all is illusion? Nevertheless, here you are, discussing illusion..."

Therefore, for followers of Evolian philosophy, an active and intentional approach is preferred over quietist Vedāntism. This perspective values

Actionism, which involves shaping the world positively through willpower and vision, rather than the passive idealism characteristic of Vedanta.

This illustrates Evola's position in the debate against Guénon's Vedāntist approach.

Nevertheless, Vedānta as a whole is not entirely without merit. It is theistic and incorporates the concept of God within its system in a significant manner. An eternal light permeates it; essential reality is viewed as *Lux Aeterna*, with a spark of this eternal light present in each of us. Vedānta posits that we are influenced by God and are part of God; this encapsulates the essence of Vedānta. The Vedantic scholar Śankara also taught that God manifests in various forms depending on the student's esoteric proficiency and spiritual perspective; however, underlying all these manifestations is an eternal, sublime reality. The personal realization of this sublime reality is the individual soul, or ātman. Conversely, when a philosophical school such as Buddhism denies the eternal light and proposes a world composed not of eternal souls but of randomly associated particles, it encounters intellectual inconsistencies. Evola was more influenced by Buddhism than by Vedāntic theism.

Evola did not support the concepts of the soul or reincarnation, nor did he recognize any form of divine influence.

This concept must be acknowledged. Actionism, as interpreted through Evola's philosophy, advocates for theistic principles and emphasizes divine influxus and the enduring light within each individual.

The friendly debate between Evola and Guénon concerning the viability of Vedānta should not be overstated; it should not be viewed as a *zero-sum game*. For instance, Evola himself recognized the value of a document such as the Bhagavad-Gītā, which is foundational to Vedānta. Evola demonstrated an appreciation for the serene and devout warrior, anchored in the divine, as an enduring ideal, as evidenced in his work *Metaphysics of War.*

The Heroic East

Evola aimed to present India, the Hindu East, in a distinct manner. His intention was not to depict the conventional East, but rather a unique perspective: "the great, heroic East, not that of Theosophists, humanitarian pantheists or old gentlemen in rapture before the various Gandhis and Rabindranath Tagores"... [Evola 2011, p. 47]

In the title essay of *Metaphysics of War*, Evola presents his interpretation of the Bhagavad-Gītā. Although this topic has been previously discussed, this iteration offers a slightly different perspective.

He praises the heroic kṣatriya dharma aspect of the Bhagavad-Gītā, unlike others who focus on its pious side, both in Evola's time and today.

Evola appropriately commends the Bhagavad-Gītā as an advocate of action. It emphasizes the purity of heroic action, "which must be wanted for itself, beyond every contingent motivation, every passion, and all gross utility" [p. 82].

Evola, an atheist, references the Bhagavad-Gītā to discuss the concept of the immortality of the soul and the necessity of divine guidance in combat. According to Evola, the hero embodies the divine, fighting for dharma, disregarding death, and yearning for a just conflict as prescribed in the Bhagavad-Gītā. Evola asserts that this perspective aligns with Tradition, while pacifism lacks any traditional foundation and is merely an expression of materialist nihilism.

This is the Evolian Bhagavad-Gītā.

The Bhagavad-Gītā, in the context of kṣatriya dharma, can be compared to the Grail saga as an embodiment of warrior asceticism. In the Bhagavad-Gītā, a deity imparts his teachings not to a priest but to a warrior, which Julius Evola describes as the path of sacred heroism and absolute action. This interpretation contrasts with the mainstream view of the Bhagavad-Gītā, which tends to emphasize serene devotion.

Evola's interpretation of the Bhagavad-Gītā, which presents a Rigorist-Actionist perspective, is quite distinctive.

The Actionist Evola

We previously mentioned that Evola regarded the Bhagavad-Gītā as a doctrine of action. Earlier in this chapter, we characterized our interpretation of Evola's philosophy as Actionist, which is grounded in our own theory known as Actionism. In 2017, this theoretical framework was published under the title *Actionism – How to Become a Responsible Man*. This work includes a chapter that presents an Actionist perspective on a significant portion of Evola's oeuvre.

Below is a summary of the "actionist" aspects of Evola's philosophy. By allowing Evola to shed light on our principles, we may also gain new insights into his own doctrines.

In *Ride the Tiger*, Evola emphasizes the importance of deliberate action. In these challenging times, characterized by atheism and nihilism, retreating from the world to live as a secluded contemplative is not a viable option. Continuous meditation does not yield the same results today as it did in more reflective eras. Currently, everything is influenced by politics, and neutrality is no longer feasible. Choosing to live as a traditional hermit, dedicated to meditation and the study of ancient scriptures, also constitutes a political statement. Therefore, it is preferable to explicitly take a political stance, oppose the nihilist regime, and engage with its materialist foundation. By enduring its challenges until they subside, one can ultimately overcome it.

Evola's philosophy, as discussed in *Tiger* and similarly advocated in *Actionism*, emphasizes the necessity of action. No individual can be entirely passive, including those who meditate in seclusion. Activities such as breathing and drinking water are still actions. While a recluse might lead a relatively tranquil life, complete inactivity is impossible. Given that we all must engage in some form of action, particularly in an era marked by pervasive propaganda (as detailed in my work *Astral War*, 2023), it is imperative for a mindful individual to participate in politics and oppose the nihilistic forces exerting control over our lives.

In *Tiger*, Evola critiqued Nietzsche on the basis of mindfulness. This discussion is reproduced in *Borderline* (2016). According to Evola, if a superman can be created, he must embody mindfulness. This concept aligns with Actionism, which refers to the superman as "the Responsible Man." The idea is that having God within a mindful person, termed the Aristocrat of the Soul or the Responsible Man, allows one to disregard traditional moral rules and act according to the essence of things.

The Actionist principle can be encapsulated as "Act Not On The Thing But On The Soul Of The Thing." Julius Evola, in his writings, highlighted the concept of the "god inside" found in the Hindu phrase "aham brahmāsmi," as a method for responsible living devoid of titanic aspirations. [Evola 2009, p. 71] Similarly, Actionism promotes a supermanist approach towards life.

Moreover, Evola's doctrine presents an optimistic outlook, which aligns with the principles of Actionism. Actionism emphasizes "Winning As Propensity," resonating with the author of *Ride the Tiger* by highlighting the inevitable decline of empires from a political perspective, and with *Meditations on the Peaks* by underscoring mountaineering as a strengthening activity on a personal level.

Actionism grounds itself on the principle of Memento Mori, which aligns with Heidegger's concept of "Sein-zum-Tode," emphasizing the acknowledgment of our finite lifespans. Similarly, Evola, in his work *Metaphysics of War*, frequently references the Bhagavad-Gītā, which describes a warrior who either ascends to heaven upon death in battle or survives to rule a kingdom. This notion of equanimity towards death [Bg 2.37-38] encapsulates the essence of Memento Mori.

To further illustrate Evola's Memento Mori perspective: as discussed in Chapter Two, after World War I, Evola experienced thoughts of suicide. However, after reading a Buddhist text that suggested viewing suicide as an act of indulgence, he was able to overcome these thoughts. This approach exemplifies the "Memento Mori Mindset" of Actionism, where one acknowledges mortality without recklessly pursuing it.

CHAPTER FIFTEEN

This study consistently revisits the ethos of ancient Rome, characterized by an elevated and dignified atmosphere. The concepts of *gravitas, dignitas,* and *contemptus* encapsulate this essence. In doing so, we aim to articulate the unique perspective of Evolian thought.

Italy may currently be regarded as a mere symbol of historical significance, reflecting its past glory and grandeur. The Roman Empire, which originated in Italy, has faded into history. Presently, the leading influence is held by the northern, industrial powers.

Nevertheless, Italy and the essence of *Romanità* continue to exert a subtle influence. Consider the Western film genre as an illustrative example.

The Western genre, which originated in the USA along with its film industry, experienced a decline in popularity by the early 1960s after its peak had passed.

However, a revival was imminent – in Italy of all places. American culture had permeated Italy after World War II. While this influx could be criticized as "cultural imperialism," there was one endearing aspect to it. Aspiring filmmaker Sergio Leone, born in Italy in 1929, was captivated by the vivid imagery and cinematic quality of Western movies imported from directors such as Howard Hawks and John Ford. Leone's creative vision flourished, and upon reaching professional maturity, he produced a classic Western filmed in Italy and Spain, featuring one American lead actor alongside European performers. He also enlisted his former schoolmate Ennio Morricone to compose a simple yet evocative score.

The result was *A Fistful of Dollars*, released in 1964. In Italian, it was titled *Per un pugno di dollari*. Although it has identifiable influence from a particular Kurosawa film, it possesses a distinct style characterized by restraint and pathos. The film is set in a vaguely defined southwestern region of the United States, though it is more accurately described as a fictional or universal setting. It exemplifies pure drama and cinema, embodying the essence of film art.

The grandeur of it all is implicitly Roman. Under Leone's direction, the actors embody Roman profundity and dignity—*gravitas* and *dignitas,* even *contemptus* – in how the two main heroes behave.

To connect this to the current argument, it can be asserted that Evola was akin to Leone in the realm of 20th century thought. Much like his counterpart in the film industry, Evola introduced gravitas, dignitas, and contemptus to an audience largely unfamiliar with these concepts. In the post-1945 cultural landscape characterized by talkative heroes, jesting clowns, continuous music, and pervasive laughter across all artistic and intellectual forms, both Evola and Leone, through their inherent nature and presence, imparted a distinctive atmosphere. This atmosphere was one of desolate plazas, solemn music, enduring gazes, and prolonged silence. The mood of empty plazas, funeral music, "long-lasting gazes, and long-lasting silence".

The particular quotation is derived from Evola's *Pagan Imperialism* and serves as an ideal link between him and Leone. Evola sought an alternative to the contemporary world characterised by chaotic noise and fleeting impressions. Similarly, Leone allowed silence to convey meaning in many of his scenes. His films incorporated a unique element of silent moments, expressionless faces, and prolonged stares.

This atmosphere of gravitas, dignitas, and contemptus undoubtedly requires a Roman origin and influence.

Italians generally possess an aesthetic sensibility that surpasses that of Americans. Rooted in Stoicism, as exemplified by Evola and Leone, this sensibility manifests in a distinctive and refined aesthetic.

This illustrates the significance of culture and tradition, of the "echoes in ancient valves." Italians, particularly those from Rome (like Leone and Evola), possess an innate sense of style and gravitas. Residing in a city sculpted by ancient and Renaissance artistry has a profound influence, even if only subtly through indirect exposure.

The Evolian Style

Leaving Leone behind, we now focus on Evola in a preliminary attempt at a summation. With his Italian-Roman influence and his artistic background in painting and poetry, Evola made a significant impact. While his "an-ātman, no gods" perspective might have been a limitation, Guénon was more comprehensive in this respect. However, the Frenchman did not always match the level of style and readability that Evola achieved at times. Although Evola's major works may not be highly engaging, he also had the ability to write popular texts for periodicals. Examples of this are found in *Meditations on the Peaks* and the foreword to Codreanu's *The Prison Notes*, which exhibit characteristics of travelogues and reports of his experiences and observations.

Having a thorough understanding of how to present your case in an accessible manner significantly enhances the overall quality of the work, particularly if you are as knowledgeable as Evola.

The aforementioned works, including *Metaphysics of War* and the memoir *The Path of Cinnabar,* are among Evola's most accessible writings. These can serve as an introduction to his other works. While *Rivolta* may be somewhat formal, many of his other books, such as those on the Grail and *Ride the Tiger,* are more approachable for educated readers. Additionally, *Pagan Imperialism* is notable for its impactful opening pages, which Evola referred to as an "angry little book." This essay makes a significant statement in its initial section, which sets the tone for the rest of the work.

Raymond Chandler's dictum is: "the word is *gusto*". Evola captures that spirit in his finest essays.

Evola in Nuce

Evola perceived the world not as an illusion or an intellectual exercise, but as an embodiment of power. Similar to Nietzsche at his most insightful, Evola developed a doctrine that was not reliant on literature, modern thought, or theoretical concepts; instead, he embodied Tradition itself. His perspective was one that eschewed conventional theories and values, focusing instead on elemental forces and primordial meanings.

This encapsulates Evola's approach. His objective is to transcend contemporary jargon, including the terminology of erudition and scholarship, and surpass conventional ways of expression. Similarly, Jünger in his work *Der Arbeiter* aimed for a perspective that transcends common concepts such as "Europe, industrialism, Goethe, Shakespeare." In a commentary, he suggested that a new terminology, hinting at eternal myth and tradition along with some newly created terms, should be employed to convey his vision.

Evola referred to "meta-historical" and "supra-historical" concepts when discussing Hyperborea, Tradition, and Uranian perspectives. This approach can transform the essay form into a sophisticated medium, a speculative method also utilized by figures such as Guido von List, Rudolf Gorsleben, and Miguel Serrano. A refined, conceptually bold presentation is essential to reach that elusive realm of "forces, powers, and primordial meanings." This is the domain of Nietzsche, who epitomized *Stilwille,* or the "will to style" — an individual who transcended conventional literature to express life itself through essays. Nietzsche even departed from the traditional essay format once to write in a fictional style, as exemplified in Zarathustra.

Evola's work didn't create a fictional impact, but his artistic talent infused his prose with timeless wisdom, myth, and history. He revived conservatism through timeless myth and authored the myth of the 21st century. His influence is just beginning to emerge.

CHAPTER SIXTEEN

PARALLEL LIVES: EVOLA AND JÜNGER

In 2014, I published a well-received biography titled *Ernst Jünger – A Portrait.*

The book you are currently reading follows a similar structure to the Jünger book: it includes some biographical information at the beginning, an analysis of central works, and concludes with conceptual discussions.

Evola and Jünger share several significant similarities. Both were born in the late 19th century and passed away before the conclusion of the 20th century. They have become prominent figures in the realm of radical conservatism in the 21st century, and their literary works are increasingly gaining popularity.

What similarities do they share, and what distinguishes them? Using their life stories as a framework, the following observations can be made.

To begin with, it is evident that they were aware of each other. Evola mentioned Jünger's *Storm of Steel* in *Metaphysics of War,* and referenced *The Worker* in a later essay. In summary, he appreciated the former but offered some criticism of the latter. However, we will not delve further into this debate, as Evola had a tendency to critique many things, including his fellow right-wing thinkers. Instead, we will present an overview of the two individuals in a more flexible manner.

Both Ernst Jünger and Julius Evola were European, with Jünger being German and Evola Italian. They experienced the tranquility of pre-war Europe during their formative years. Their studies were interrupted by World War I, leading both to serve as officers in the army reserve. During the 1920s, Jünger became notable for his war-related writings and emerged as a celebrated figure in the otherwise bleak Weimar culture. In contrast, Evola's wartime experiences were less noteworthy, and he did not emphasize them as prominently. Nevertheless, Evola also served as an artillery officer and remained in the army reserve like Jünger. Although Evola sought to rejoin the military ranks during World War II, his request was denied.

During the 1920s and 1930s, Evola and Jünger were both keen observers of their era and its impact on humanity and society. Jünger expanded his repertoire to include belles-lettres, writing essays and eventually a novel (*Auf den Marmorklippen*), which earned him recognition among literary audiences. In contrast, Evola maintained a more academic approach in his writings. It is important to note that in the 1910s and 1920s, Evola had begun his career as a visual artist and authored an essay on art, as well as occasionally engaging in poetry. Thus, during the interwar period, both individuals evolved into style-conscious authors who exhibited *Stilwille*.

Both individuals interacted with their respective totalitarian regimes—Fascist and National Socialist. They managed to avoid being entirely consumed by these regimes, maintaining their own perspectives on radical conservatism and tradition while delineating the extent of the regimes' influence on their personal views.

This culminated in WWII. Both individuals survived, although Evola was left partially paralyzed due to injuries from the Viennese bomb raid, and Jünger experienced the loss of his eldest son, Ernstel, who was killed in action in November 1944 in Carrara, Italy.

In the post-war period, there is a slight divergence between the two figures. Jünger, while not entirely mainstream, became well-known as a conservative author and was awarded the prestigious Goethe Prize in 1982, indicating significant recognition. Conversely, Evola remained a staunch radical, and his influence on right-wing movements even led to legal proceedings against him for inciting rebellion.

Nevertheless, they shared similar perspectives. Jünger discussed the concept of resisting mass society by becoming a forest walker in his work *Der Waldgänger* (1951). Similarly, Evola emphasized the spiritual significance of mountain climbing in his book *Meditations on the Peaks* (1974). He contrasted the communal, materialistic nature of downhill skiing, which relies on ski lifts, with the more solitary and self-reliant pursuit of climbing, which requires one to elevate oneself both mentally and physically.

There were additional similarities.

Towards the end of their lives, both Jünger and Evola exhibited notable foresight in their perspectives.

In his 1990s diary, Jünger anticipated divine occurrences. He believed the 20th century was dominated by Titans, characterized by forces of nihilism and regimentation that led humanity into states of constant labor without leisure. In contrast, he envisioned the deities of the 21st century as Olympian in nature—musical, just, and compassionate powers guiding humanity towards prosperous, water-rich valleys. However, this transformation would only be possible if individuals possessed an intrinsic nature aligned with these values, displaying an esoteric quality of willing goodness, light, and truth. As a follower of Goethe, Jünger consistently emphasized that, ultimately, "it is decided within" – *I'm Innern ist's getan.*

Jünger conveyed a thoughtful message. In a similar vein, Evola expressed that the forces of nihilism are not sustainable and that the Kali Yuga must eventually conclude. The mindful rebel, recognizing the prevailing materialism, defeatism, and self-loathing, should not merely withdraw from society. Instead, he should maintain some level of engagement with the world, metaphorically riding the tiger's back. When this metaphorical tiger is completely exhausted and the forces of nihilism have dissipated, the mindful rebel ought to step in and assume responsibility.

Both visions, whether it is the return of the gods or the concept of riding the tiger, reflect an optimistic outlook. While they recognize the current challenges facing the world, they also envision future possibilities and a brighter day ahead for thoughtful, perceptive, and conscientious individuals, referred to here as the Aristocrats of the Soul.

The progression into the 21st century marks a transition from the lingering influences of Kali Yuga to the emerging realities of Dvāpara Yuga across various aspects. Both Jünger and Evola have acknowledged this shift.

Regarding parallel lives, Carlos Castaneda also comes to mind. He and Evola had similarities. This South American shaman has been mentioned previously.

Firstly, both Evola and Castaneda were interested in the "warrior ways of enlightenment". They emphasized the concept of "the warrior" as a symbol of mindful striving. As Castaneda states in his first book: "A man goes to knowledge as he goes to war – wide awake, with fear, with respect, and with absolute determination of purpose." [Castaneda 1990, p. 52] This sentiment aligns with Evola's perspective. Similarly, this was referenced earlier with regards to Evola's *Metaphysics of War*, which discusses such mindful warrior attitudes comprehensively.

In *The Yoga of Power*, Evola discussed the Tantric path to wisdom, which is a rigorous process of self-realization. According to Evola, "delusions, adversities, personal tragedies and failures, even catastrophes may play the role of a hidden guru, of a spiritual teacher sui generis; they may be interpreted as signs to discern the right path." [Evola 1992, p. 95]. This concept is similar to Castaneda's teacher Don Juan, who said: "[L]ife is an endless challenge, and challenges cannot possibly be good or bad. Challenges are simply challenges." [Castaneda 1974, p. 108]

Julius Evola suggested the necessity of transcending the human condition, advocating for a connection to the realm of *apauruṣeya*, where communication with gods is possible. Similarly, in *The Eagle's Gift*, Castaneda describes shamanist disciples as reaching a point in their training where "they cease to be persons and the human condition is no longer part of their view." [Castaneda 1981, p. 308]

✠

A final relevant example of "parallel lives" in relation to Evola is his association with his acknowledged mentor, René Guénon.

Guénon was about 12 years older than Evola, but we will focus on their similarities. Today, both figures are experiencing a resurgence of interest, often regarded as significant scholars. However, during their lifetimes, they were considered outsiders and radicals. Evola, due to his opposition to Christianity and Catholicism, held a marginalized position in Italian society. Similarly, Guénon, despite his writing style reflecting "transparency, *Académie Française*, Latin European intellectualism," was viewed as a heretic and an unorthodox thinker. Because of this, he had to flee the country and live in Egypt; that was his own explanation of becoming an exile.

In summary, both Evola and Guénon were esteemed scholars of esoteric traditions during an era marked by pervasive nihilism. Although they were considered marginal figures within their respective national societies, their erudition and eloquence were unmistakable. Meticulous in their style and demeanour, they were nonetheless perceived as challengers to the status quo.

The history of their 20th-century ideas and thought must be remembered.

CHAPTER SEVENTEEN

The terms "metaphysical," "tradition," and "traditional" are often used interchangeably in Evola's writing.

This occasionally made his vocabulary vague.

When capturing Leviathan, it is not always possible to be meticulous. Describing man's situation during the dawn of Dvāpara yuga can be seen as an art form. Evola possessed traits of a meticulous intellectual, but he was not aligned with the critical approach of the Frankfurt school. He was known for his mystical and artistic inclinations, combined with a unique terminology. Using terms like *Uranian, Telluric, Hyperborean, metaphysical, tradition, metahistorical, suprahistorical, neorealism*, and others, he established a distinct position in the intersection of history, myth, philosophy, religion, and art.

The central focus of Evola's work is on Tradition.

Let us take a final look at Tradition and its counterpart: the pervasive issue of today, the global culture of nihilism and materialism.

What, therefore, constitutes anti-Tradition?

I would state the following: The absence of recognition for a human soul, or eternal values rooted in Will, Thought, and Compassion, as well as the disregard for eternal ideas (Greek *eidos*, plural, *eidoi*) that give form to matter, can be described as nihilism or materialism. This perspective appears to dominate contemporary Western society, which is facing challenges such as moral and cultural decline. Failure to acknowledge either Will, eternal *eidoi*, or enduring values reflects a state of decadence, indicating a potential exhaustion of mental, conceptual, and cultural vitality.

To merely concentrate on economic growth and remain blind to spiritual qualities is nihilism, which equates to materialism and/or decadence.

A culture that rules its citizens through entertainment and fear-based propaganda is a decadent culture.

A culture where teachers use agenda-driven rhetoric and overlook metaphysical truths is a decadent culture.

A culture fighting constant wars to create fear in the citizens is a decadent culture.

A culture praising sex workers and addicts is a decadent culture.

However, there is a solution to all this: Tradition. It encompasses more than just "reading the classics, promoting fiscal conservatism, donning a Fedora, and smiling smugly."

Tradition, as first highlighted by Guénon, extends beyond contemporary understanding to ancient origins in regions like Hyperborea. This idea traces back to human history in the polar regions, referred to as *Midgard, Paradesha, Thule,* Śveta-Dvīpa, *Ariyanem Vaejah.* It suggests a foundational spiritual order that influences the world over time. Cultural and spiritual patterns observed in China, India, the Middle East, and Europe indicate potential roots in northern polar regions, suggesting a culture of regality and sacrality illuminated by the Northern Star. The rotation of Ursa Major around the star forms a significant symbolic cross, representing a beacon for future developments.

We aim to cultivate a culture grounded in spirituality, consistently opposing materialism at all times.

We will create a culture that is serious, dignified, and dismissive of the trivial chatter prevalent in today's mainstream.

We aim to foster a culture that celebrates individuals who contribute positively to society through moral values and personal development, rather than those who pursue self-indulgent behaviors.

We will foster a culture filled with temples, churches, palaces, and grand loggias, as well as Viking halls and mead halls—architectural creations that stand the test of time. We aim to avoid the monstrosities of glass and chrome cluttered with neon signs advertising peep shows, movie theaters, and fast-food establishments that provide the public with low-quality offerings—junk food and junk culture.

It is enough...!

The world is poised for change. A new era led by Responsible Men, rooted in Tradition and ancient myths, will replace the current pessimistic rulers. These new leaders will be spiritually enlightened and worthy of their title.

The tree will blossom, the sick king will heal, and a new Grail King will ascend. *This myth is about to unfold, becoming the story of our times.* Evola and Guénon have shown the way. Now it's up to you to live it, envision it, and make it real.

CHAPTER EIGHTEEN

This section contains fragments and insights from the study that didn't fit into the structured chapters but still hold value.

Downsides of Evola

Evola's approach had several notable limitations: he advocated for the concept of *an*-ātman (no gods), and he dismissed all modern scientific advancements, including Goethean holistic science. Additionally, he failed to recognize the unity of will and thought, focusing solely on the aspect of will within this duality.

Core Quote

I am currently unable to locate the source of this quote by Evola. However, it succinctly encapsulates his *modus operandi*, reflecting the mindset of a traditionalist involved in contemporary politics:

"Be radical, have principles, be absolute, be that which the bourgeoisie calls an extremist: give yourself without counting or calculating, don't accept what they call 'the reality of life' and act in such a way that you won't be accepted by that kind of 'life,' never abandon the principle of struggle."

Pure, Hard, Certain

Pur, dur, sûr – "pure, hard, certain". This is a French proverb that fits Evola rather well.

Death of Affect

Jim Ballard's perspective on fiction writing involves the concept of the "death of affect" as it relates to character development. This principle suggests that writers should refrain from sentimentalizing their characters and avoid manipulating the reader's emotions by portraying protagonists as overly perfect or morally impeccable. By adopting this approach, authors can create more authentic and engaging characters, thereby enhancing the narrative's overall impact and relevance.

Similarly, Evola adopts this attitude towards ethics, promoting an anti-emotionalism stance. This approach, which can be described as the "death of affect as a modus operandi in ethics," emphasizes the importance of maintaining objectivity and emotional detachment in ethical considerations.

The Acerbic Evola

The critical perspective of Evola highlights examples of the Roman ideal of *contemptus* within our esteemed subject. He opposed the Italian cultural mainstream, as seen in his work *Men Among the Ruins*, p. 257: "the trivial Italy of mandolins, museums, 'O Sole Mio,' and the tourist industry".

The Tantric Nietzsche

In *The Yoga of Power*, Evola asserts that there are some parallels between Tantrism and Nietzschean philosophy. He describes Tantra as a doctrine of the mindful superman. According to Evola, the Tantric *sādhana* (spiritual path or discipline) aligns with Nietzsche's assertion that "man is something that must be overcome," but with greater seriousness [Evola 1992, p. 16]. Nietzsche's philosophy suggests that everything is an expression of the Will to Power, while Tantric metaphysics posits that everything is *shakti* (power). This connection underlies the doctrine of *siddhis* (superhuman powers) [ibid p. 17].

SOURCES

The online resources pertinent to this study are listed as follows.

Chapter Two discusses Evola's association with Maria de Naglowska. For further information, please refer to the following online source: [https://www.fyinpaper.com/julius-evola-and-maria-de-neglowska/]

Chapter Two also includes a quote from Evola's diary of 1943, which details his journey to Germany during that year. The relevant online source can be found at: [https://evolaasheis.wordpress.com/2016/04/14/diary-1943-1944-excerpt/]

Chapter Four examines Evola's essay *Arte Astratta*. An English translation, featuring selected color reproductions of his oil paintings, is titled *Dada*, sine loco et anno. It is available online at the following link: [https://archive.org/details/dada-julius-evola/page/n1/mode/2up]

In the same chapter, the poem "The Obscure Dialogue of the Inner Landscape" is presented.

The source for this poem is: [https:/
evolaasheis.wordpress.com/2016/04/14/
the-obscure-dialogue-of-the-inner-landscape/]

Chapter Four includes the poem "opus 32",
translated into English by Olivia Sears. The source of
this translation can be found at:
 [https://www.catranslation.org/
blog-post/a-post-dada-superfascist-shadow/].

At the end of Chapter Six, I reference Evola's text "The
Sacred in the Roman Tradition". You can find it here:
[https://evolaasheis.wordpress.com/2016/04/14/
the-sacred-in-the-roman-tradition/]

Finally, Chapter Fourteen reviews Evola's "A
Controversy About the Vedanta". The text is
available online here: [https://evolaasheis.wordpress.
com/2018/03/01/a-controversy-about-the-Vedanta/]

LITERATURE

Castaneda, Carlos. *The Eagle's Gift*. New York: Simon and Schuster, 1981

.- *Tales of Power*. New York: Simon & Shuster, 1974

.- *The Teachings of Don Juan*. London: Arkana, 1990

de Turris, Gianfranco. *Julius Evola: The Philosopher and Magician in War: 1943–1945*. Rochester, VT: Inner Traditions, 2020

Evola, Julius. *Meditations on the Peaks: mountain climbing as metaphor for the spiritual quest* (Meditazioni delle vette, 1974). Rochester, VT: Inner Traditions, 1998

.- *Men Among the Ruins: post-war reflections of a radical traditionalist* (Gli uomini e le rovine, 1952, 1974). Rochester, VT: Inner Traditions, 2002

.- *Metaphysics of War: battle, victory and death in the world of tradition* (2007). London: Arktos Media, 2011

.- *Pagan Imperialism* (*Imperialismo pagano*, 1928, 1933). Sine loco: Gornahoor Press, 2017

.- *Revolt Against the Modern World: politics, religion and social order of the Kali Yuga* (*Rivolta contro il mondo moderno*, 1934, 1969). Rochester, VT: Inner Traditions, 1995

.- *Ride the Tiger: a survival manual for the Aristocrats*

of the Soul (*Cavalcare le tigre*, 1961). Rochester, VT: Inner Traditions, 2003

.- *The Mystery of the Grail: initiation and magic in the quest for the Spirit* (*Il mistero del Graal*, 1937, 1994). Rochester, VT: Inner Traditions, 1997

.- *The Path of Cinnabar: an intellectual autobiography* (*Il cammino del cinabro*, 1963). London: Integral Tradition Publishing, 2009

.- *The Yoga of Power: Tantra, Shakti, and the secret way* (*Lo yoga della potenza: Saggio sui tantra*, 1968). Rochester, VT: Inner Traditions, 1992

Hansen, H. T. Foreword in *Evola, Julius, Men Among the Ruins: post-war reflections of a radical traditionalist*. Rochester, VT: Inner Traditions, 2002

Hägg, Göran. *Ett alldeles särskilt land – 150 år i Italien*. Stockholm: Norstedts, 2012

Svensson, Lennart. *Actionism – How to Become a Responsible Man*. Australia: Manticore Press, 2017

APPENDIX ONE

BIBLIOGRAPHY IN ITALIAN

A list of Evolian works in the form of separate publications, like books and pamphlets, with their original titles.

Arte Astratta, posizione teorica. Roma: Maglione e Strini, 1920
La parole obscure du paysage intérieur. Roma-Zurigo, Collection Dada, 1921 (as we can see this work was in French)
Saggi sull'idealismo magico. Todi-Roma, Atanòr, 1925
L'individuo e il divenire del mondo. Roma, Libreria di Scienze e Lettere, 1926
L'uomo come potenza, Todi-Roma, Atanòr, 1927
Teoria dell'individuo assoluto. Torino, Bocca, 1927
Imperialismo pagano. Todi-Roma, Atanòr, 1928
Fenomenologia dell'individuo assoluto. Torino, Bocca, 1930
La tradizione ermetica. Bari, Laterza, 1931
Maschera e volto dello spiritualismo contemporaneo. Torino, Bocca, 1932

Rivolta contro il mondo moderno. Milano, Hoepli, 1934

Tre aspetti del problema ebraico. Roma, Mediterranee, 1936

Il mistero del Graal. Bari, Laterza, 1937

Il mito del sangue. Milano, Hoepli, 1937

Indirizzi per una educazione razziale. Napoli, Conte, 1941

Sintesi di dottrina della razza. Milano, Hoepli, 1941

La dottrina del risveglio. Bari, Laterza, 1943

Lo Yoga della Potenza. Torino, Bocca, 1949

Orientamenti. Roma, Imperium, 1950

Gli uomini e le rovine. Roma, Edizioni dell'Ascia, 1953

Metafisica del sesso. Todi-Roma, Atanòr, 1958

L'«Operaio» nel pensiero di Ernst Jünger. Roma, Armando, 1959

Cavalcare la tigre. Milano, Vanni Scheiwiller, 1961

Il cammino del cinabro. Milano, Vanni Scheiwiller, 1963

Il Fascismo. Saggio di una analisi critica dal punto di vista della destra. Roma, Volpe, 1963

L'arco e la clava. Milano, Vanni Scheiwiller, 1968

Raāga Blanda. Milano, Vanni Scheiwiller, 1969

Il taoismo. Roma, Mediterranee, 1972

Ricognizioni, Uomini e problemi. Roma, Mediterranee, 1974

APPENDIX TWO

List of (mainly Italian) compilations and works mainly published after Evola's death; a selection.

Meditazioni delle vette. La Spezia, Edizioni del Tridente, 1971
Diario 1943-44. Genova, Centro Studi Evoliani, 1975
Considerazioni sulla guerra occulta. Genova, Centro Studi Evoliani, 1977
Il nichilismo attivo di Federico Nietzsche. Roma, Fondazione Julius Evola, 1978
Lo Stato. Roma, Fondazione Julius Evola, 1978
Spengler e il "Tramonto dell'Occidente". Roma, Fondazione Julius Evola, 1981
La tragedia della Guardia di Ferro. Roma, Fondazione Julius Evola, 1996
Fascismo e Terzo Reich. Roma, Mediterranee, 2001
Il "mistero iperboreo". Scritti sugli Indoeuropei 1934-1970. Roma, Fondazione Julius Evola, 2003
Ernst Jünger. Il combattente, l'operaio, l'anarca. Roma, Passaggio al Bosco, 2017

INDEX OF PERSONS (SELECTIVE)

Aleramo, Sibill,	20
Anderson, Laurie	46
Codreanu, Corneliu	22, 23, 178
Eliade, Mircea	22
Eschenbach, Wolfram von	93
Evola, Vincenzo	17
Guénon, René	9, 15, 38-41, 51, 87, 93, 96, 115, 165-168, 178, 187, 191, 192
Hansen, H. T.	22, 23, 33-35, 37, 38, 55, 59, 81
Itten, Johannes	43
Jünger, Ernst	3, 5, 6, 59, 78, 114, 126, 140, 148, 149, 156, 157, 159, 160, 163, 180-185, 202, 205
Kandinsky, Wassily	43

Leone, Sergio   7, 176-177

Marinetti, Filippo Tommaso   17, 19, 47

de Naglowska, Maria   20, 197

Nietzsche, Friedrich   5, 15, 17, 37, 38, 42, 53, 55-58, 66, 72-74, 100, 142, 148, 171, 179, 180, 195

Spengler, Oswald   15, 37, 38

ABOUT THE AUTHOR

Lennart Svensson, a native of Sweden, earned a Bachelor of Arts in Indology from Uppsala University. He commenced his career as an author in 2014 with the publication of *Ernst Jünger – A Portrait*. Since then, he has authored numerous essays in both English and Swedish, including the notable works *Ett rike utan like* and *Actionism*. His most recent essay, *Astral War*, was published in 2023.